INTERIOR ILLUSTRATIONS: Anuj Shrestha.

Printed in China

AUTHOR .... TITLE .... PAGE

RUI TENREIRO .... *New Players in an Old Field* .... COVER

LETTERS .... *from Emerson Whitney,* 8
Jose Antonio Vargas, Michelle Tea,
Kristen Iskandrian, & Mary Houlihan

JINCY WILLETT .... *Only the Lonely* 25

GENEVIEVE HUDSON .... *If We Could Stay Like This Forever* ... 39

DANTIEL W. MONIZ .... *Thicker Than Water* 51

REIF LARSEN .... *Instructions for an Expedition* 69

MICHAEL DEAGLER .... *All Addicts* 75

DAWN DAVIES .... *Music to Be Played if* 95
I Fall into a Coma

SHUBNUM KHAN .... *A World Waiting to Be Lived In* 117

T. C. BOYLE .... *The Apartment* 131

NEW NIGERIAN VOICES

CHIMAMANDA NGOZI ADICHIE ... *Introduction* 155

OPE ADEDEJI .... *After the Birds* 157

ROY UDEH-UBAKA .... *Until It Doesn't* 173

ADACHIOMA EZEANO .... *Becoming the Baby Girl* 191

CHUKWUEBUKA IBEH .... *The Good Ones Are Not Here* 211

NGOZI JOHN .... *Fading Lights* 229

THREE POEMS BY DANIIL KHARMS
TRANSLATED BY KATIE FARRIS & ILYA KAMINSKY

How a Man Crumbles; *A Man Falls Asleep*; *Sonnet* 50, 74, 130

DEAR McSWEENEY'S,

I have two kinds of nightmares these days. In one, somebody spikes a drink of mine or tricks me into doing drugs, something I haven't done in years. In the other I get a bad tattoo. Usually, it's on my chest and something cartoonish like a rainbow pony. Permanence: permanence is the subject of both nightmares, permanence and bad decisions. I hate the idea of being pigeonholed. When you look up the definition of the word online, one of the first images that comes up is clip art of a box for multiple pigeons, with wooden compartments, each about the size of a bird. The birds are standing sort of listlessly, looking around, with barely enough room to pivot.

I want to write about this stuff even though I'm afraid to be permanently here.

I had a dream a few nights ago that I still had boobs—they were hairy, significantly hairy, around my nipples, like little shaggy dogs. I was okay with them in the dream. I had the breasts and my scar lines, both.

There's nowhere to go.

Except these days I live near Hollywood, and the other day I went out for an open casting call on a whim. I have zero acting aspirations, but the woman who'd advertised the call was trans, and she'd said something like "Everybody's complaining that they're using cis people in trans roles. You have the chance to change that." I *had* been complaining about that; it felt like she was talking to me. I read the description. The casting agency was looking for non-passing, trans masculine people who look nineteen—me. I'm thirty-two. So I shoved aside all the papers I was supposed to grade, and in the shower I memorized the few lines we were supposed to. I drove to Burbank with a clean shirt.

The place was in an office park. I knew a handful of people in the waiting room. Trans folks were practicing with the wall, the water fountain. I hadn't really practiced aside from my moment in the shower, but this was an experiment. I got a mug of water from the kitchen in the office, and when they called me I walked into the taping with my mug. The two ladies in the room behind the camcorder looked at each other and said, "That's great" before I could do much. They gave me the business card for an agent—"You should get one," they said. "Raw talent."

It was a total lie and I knew it, but I figured maybe I should turn it into a writing project. See what I could report about it, explore tokenism at this level. So I went to the agency and brought a poem I'd written and memorized long ago. I just wanted to see where it would go. I shrugged thinking about it.

When I met with the guys, it was in a dusty office off Wilshire with fans going in every window. It felt like dragnet. There were stress balls everywhere and wire trash cans filled with balled paper. They asked me to perform in front of a table with four computers on it and a little bookshelf with a handful of books about acting and a small brass monkey with a waving arm.

"That was good," they said when I was done, and asked me where I'd studied acting.

"Nowhere," I said. "I'm a writer."

"Sit down," they said, and started talking to me about nerds.

"Six years ago, what would we do with a nerd?"

I didn't know.

"Now, for some reason, they're selling, hard-core," they said. "We try to find the trends—your people are it right now."

At the same time as this was happening, I'd joined a trans chorus. I'd finished my first book and had time on my hands, plus I've always loved to sing. Things were fine at first. I liked meeting up with the group of twenty-five trans people once a week. I'm guilty of liking structured socialization, and despite my own embarrassment about it, I actually teared up on my first night while we sang a cheery, cheesy version of "Iris" by the Goo Goo Dolls: "And I don't want the world to see me / 'cause I don't think that they'd understand."

This was okay, seemed okay, because although there were giant billboards of Jeffrey Tambor advertising *Transparent* all over the city in advance of the second season, and even though I'd had to unsubscribe from my Google Alerts for the term *transgender*—because since 2011 (when I'd set it) the articles using the term had spiked uproariously, to the point that it was a slog to get through my inbox, hundreds of articles every few days—I thought maybe I should participate in all of this. I kept feeling like I should, kept getting pangs of jealousy whenever a trans person who fit my description was getting attention for something, their art, anything, really. Lists sprang up: "Most Important Trans People in [This Subject Area]"; "Ten Trans People to Know in 2015"; "Trans Change-Makers"; "Trans Poets"; "The Hottest Trans Masc, QTPOC Folks from the Internet"; et cetera.

I felt the same way when I saw *It Takes Two* with the Olsen twins and one of them was butch and played stickball and I wanted to kill her for being me and not being me. Fuck her, my eight-year-old self was thinking. That's me, or close enough to me to hurt. My childhood self was fondling competitiveness, terminal uniqueness, and turning it around in my mouth. I was angered by someone who served as a representative of my most visible attribute—androgyny?—showing up in the media, because it felt like my cultural stamp. Because capitalism ensures that we occupy spaces through categorization, my thinking was that "me" had

already been made. It was finished. They did me already. No more room. The musical chairs of identity and appearance dictate that there's one slot for a person of color, one for a disabled kid, and maybe, in the last five or ten years, a queer, almost always a white, "able-bodied" one.

Trans choir got weird quickly. We were soon followed by a camera crew during every practice, the music got more and more "widely appealing," the leadership was most excited about potential TV performances and started to articulate a trajectory aimed at HBO specials and corporate sponsors.

"You are the Trans Chorus of Los Angeles. Not the Trans Chorus of the Inland Empire or the Trans Chorus of Orange County... YOU are the Trans Chorus of Los Angeles. You are in the second largest market in our country and you DEFINITELY sit in the city with the largest soapbox and the loudest megaphone to shout the message of equality to the freakin' rooftops! We WILL play at the Hollywood Bowl, we will play at Rockefeller Center, we WILL be on The Ellen Show and Oprah Show and blah, blah, blah [sic]— THIS is where we're going!" wrote a (cisgender) board member in an email to all of us toward the end of the first season.

Back in 2010, I'd been interviewed by some random cis person at ESPN who said to me that trans was at a tipping point. I'd laughed about him and this idea with my friends after I hung up the phone. Tipping point? I was living in a rural place with one other trans person. We were the only "out" queers for miles, nothing tipping—nothing new tipping, at least. There've been trans people forever, and media storms (about white, wealthy trans people) have happened in the US before.

Media trends are interesting things.

The same week that the board member's email was sent out, my friend forwarded to me a *New York Times* article with a graphic of baby things on a gradient of pink and blue, a sweeping "Charlie" across the blended purple in the middle.

IS HAYDEN A BOY OR GIRL? BOTH. 'POST-GENDER' BABY NAMES ARE ON THE RISE. Charlie, Emerson, and other unisex names are not just a Hollywood fad but a rising trend among American parents, it said.

"OMG this is you," he wrote.

That night, I was at dinner with a friend who'd worked on *Transparent* and quit. He was saying that he'd heard around that I was telling people I liked it better when they didn't pay so much attention to us. I know visibility affords so many opportunities for people who wouldn't otherwise have them, myself included, but visibility can also work as erasure, and as Miss Major says in an interview with CeCe McDonald in *Trap Door: Trans Cultural Production and the Politics of Visibility*, mainstream visibility can make life even more dangerous for the most marginalized in our community by triggering a transphobic backlash: "Another trans woman pays the price for what the media is applauding and the world is getting all happy over. There are two sides to every fucking coin."

I said that maybe trans is actually mobile and moves, and maybe will always be moving so will escape all this, and my friend said, "I think that's giving trans too much credit. Trans isn't a radical identity. It's just not." I asked about nonbinary identity.

"Maybe that one is radical," he said, and shrugged.

I quit the choir.

Love,

EMERSON WHITNEY
LOS ANGELES, CA

DEAR McSWEENEY'S,
Don't ask me where I'm from.

Don't ask me where I'm from, because I don't know. Yes, I am a grown-ass man, nearing the fifth decade of my life. And, yes, I don't know where I am from.

Simply, I can say I'm from the Philippines. I was, in fact, born there—my birth certificate says so. But aside from the clear-watered rivers where my cousins and I swam while our aunts washed clothes, I don't remember much about it. Less simply, I can say I'm from Mountain View, California, near the geographic heart of Silicon Valley. That's where my mother sent me to live with her parents. Mountain View is where I graduated from Crittenden Middle School and Mountain View High School, where I learned to speak and write "American" by reporting and writing for the local newspaper, where I realized the complication of being asked where I am from, having neither the proper papers nor the right birthplace to claim a country of my own. Mountain View is where I realized I had to run away from where I was from, wherever the running away would take me.

The journey of running away took me to Philadelphia and Washington, DC, and New York City. The journey took me to a psychological mind-set of running away not only from the US government or from friends who asked too many questions ("Where's your mother?"), but also from many parts of myself. I couldn't hear—I did not want to hear—the sound of my own voice. I reported news stories in order to write about other people; my bylines were published in the *Philadelphia Daily News*, the *Washington Post*, *Rolling Stone*, the *New Yorker*. I wrote to get lost in other people's stories, until I was so lost I didn't know who I had become. Finally, in search of myself, I read. I discovered Joan Didion's *Where I Was From*, a dissection and an excavation of her native

California, to ground my exploration of my own California. I re-read James Baldwin, who writes with such piercing, penetrating truth ("You have to *decide* who you are, and force the world to deal with you, not with its *idea* of you") that he forced me to uncover my own.

And here we are.

"I do not know where I will be when you read this book," begins *Dear America: Notes of an Undocumented Citizen*, the book I had to write before I could write anything else. I wrote the book while giving myself permission to "self-deport" and leave these United States. A human being must belong somewhere, or so I was led to believe, never realizing, until I wrote the book, that belonging is not dictated by papers I don't have or laws that have not passed. Belonging is a state of my own mind, how free I allow myself to be. It took writing to make me feel seen, sane, coherent.

So don't ask me where I'm from. No matter where I am, I live in my words.

Yours,

JOSE ANTONIO VARGAS
BERKELEY, CA

DEAR McSWEENEY'S,

Yesterday I went to get an ultrasound, following up on a mammogram I got a week or so ago. I was pretty cavalier about this, having dense breasts as I do, which is a thing: the women in my family all have dense breasts, and it means that whenever you get a mammogram they can't quite *see* things clearly, like looking through a fogged-up windshield, perhaps, or a frosted one, and so I have to go back and get an ultrasound where you recline with your arms stretched above your head while a stranger squirts warm jelly (it sounds gross, but it's better than cold jelly) all over your breasts and then runs the little ultrasound wand over you, back and forth, back and forth. Medical insurance being what it is in this country (horrid), this means that even though I *know* I have dense breasts and that a regular mammogram will not provide an adequate spy into my breast tissue, I have to go through the charade of the initial, ineffective mammogram and only then can a doctor order an insurance-covered follow-up ultrasound. Am I complaining? Yes and no. I have health insurance, which is amazing. It's sooooo expensive but somehow we afford it—well, not somehow; I know how. My spouse was in the right place at the right time and plus is a hardworking Virgo with a solid middle-class work ethic plus is genderqueer or whatever so had to work super-duper hard to prove that even though they're a freak or whatever they are such an asset to their company, which they are, and now we can afford health insurance, thank you, Dashiell.

Can I interrupt this tale to tell you I'm writing this in a café in Los Angeles and the person sitting next to me just name-dropped Jesse Tyler Ferguson, one of the gays from *Modern Family*, on the business call they are on right now? They just hung up with a director they are *really* excited to be working with; they really clicked over an *I Love Lucy* reference. This happens all the time in Los Angeles, of course, and it is so preferable to San Francisco, where everyone really is talking about tech companies all around you at restaurants and cafés, you can't escape it, and even if someone is quiet they're wearing a Google T-shirt or something. I like

this better. I actually saw Jesse Tyler Ferguson at Intelligentsia Coffeebar one day, just sitting and talking to a friend outside. My spouse and I once went on a date to this little French restaurant where we were seated right by Jenny Slate, who is my spouse's "hall pass" or whatever, but my spouse was going through this big allergy flare-up and their lips swelled out *so big* while we were sitting there, just huge and crazy like the worst joke of a bad lip job, and I felt bad for them, face-to-face with their celebrity crush, which really hardly ever happens to anyone, even here in LA, and they were having this terrible face issue. But the next time we were there the room was empty save for us and a writer from that show *Mozart in the Jungle*, which I watched only once but couldn't get too into, and the writer talked loudly about their life and it was impossible not to listen, so my spouse and I sat quietly eating our *frites* just listening to this person's life. He name-dropped another TV writer and what is so funny is that on our *next* date we were, at a different restaurant, seated next to *that* TV writer! If I'm making it sound like

14

you can move to Los Angeles and dine around television people all the time, it's because you can, but don't think that that means it's easy to make it in Hollywood or anything, because I am here to tell you that it is not.

So, back at my follow-up ultrasound, I realize that I was called back not because of dense breasts per se but because there was *something* on my initial mammogram. Something that wasn't on the last one. So they needed to do the ultrasound with the warm jelly, and the woman just keeps digging and digging and sliding the wand over this one area and I guess that's where the *something* is. And I start crying. I can't believe it. Thankfully, it's just a few tears and the woman is very intent on the screen she is staring into but now I am thinking that I am going to die and I have a four-year-old and this now makes dying terrible, awful, the worst. And I can't stop thinking about it, I'm flooded with tragic vibes. I *know* that chances are it's actually nothing, and that even if it's something chances are that that something is nothing, and even if the something is something, it's probably benign, and even if it is

not benign chances are I will survive, like the breast cancer survivors I know. The chances of this being the beginning of the end are slight, but this knowledge does not prevent me from plunging into weeping. I can't believe we're all going to die and leave behind so many unfinished projects, families, relationships. What about that guy who is suing his parents because he hadn't asked to be born and they had him for their own amusement? I love that guy; he is totally correct. I think about this all the time—that I didn't do my son any favors by birthing him into this world and what if I up and die now? I mean, what about the fact that I am going to die, if not now, eventually? How will it ever be okay?

The woman leaves the room and I wipe the warm jelly out of my armpit and off my breast with my hospital gown. I get dressed and go into the bathroom and weep. I thought it was going to be just a little teeny cry, like when they fill your coffee up too high and you need to slosh some out to add your almond milk. But I'm really crying. It takes longer than I anticipated and I leave with my sunglasses on because my face is so red and puffy. How will I be able to lie to my spouse as planned when I return home with my face all red and puffy? I've decided not to say anything until I get the results in two days. Why freak anyone out? I imagine having a secret cancer diagnosis, like the woman in *My Life Without Me*. I love that movie, though I bet I couldn't watch it now, now that I'm a mom too. I think about recording voice messages for Atti to play for the rest of his motherless life: of course I will have to do that. I don't feel the need to seduce anyone before I die, like she did, having seduced enough people, and anyway, I wouldn't have to have a cancer diagnosis to sleep with Mark Ruffalo, I think Dashiell would be understanding if that opportunity presented itself and I took advantage of it.

At home I just tell Dashiell right away as they're getting into the shower. It's Tuesday, which means our son has a longer day at school and so it's the day we have sex. I mean, we could have sex any day, sort of/ not really, but at least on Tuesday we *know* we will have sex, also get brunch, and Dashiell makes it clear that we of course do not have to have sex; we can just lie around in bed together and whatnot but *no*, I am not going to let what is not even a thing get in the way of our sex life, and plus if I am dying then I want to *live* until I die, and that means sex, lots of sex with Dashiell, but when I go into the kitchen to squash up an avocado and eat it with crackers, I can't stop crying, and even as I then eat a piece of toast with almond butter and jam, the sugar-free jam because cancer feeds on sugar, doesn't it, I can't stop crying, so then I return to Dashiell, who is taking a long shower, which means they are probably crying, too, because they pride themselves on their short showers, and I tell them I actually am too fragile to have sex. I mean, who wants to have sex with a crying person. Bummer.

We lie in bed and Dashiell essentially tells me Atti will be fine without me and even having had me as a mom for four years is such a gift. This might sound terrible to you but it is exactly what I want to hear. Dashiell and I cuddle all wound up and pretzeled and it is *so* nice because our kid sleeps between us, which means we never get to cuddle anymore and it feels so good I could fall asleep. I have a sinus cold and the crying has really exacerbated it. I decide I'll take a shower and we'll go out for food. I go into the bathroom and take off my clothes and take my dirty hair out of the bun and brush it all out so it is like a crazy clown wig, like Krusty the Clown from *The Simpsons* exactly, and in that state I return to the bedroom and tell Dashiell that from the way the woman kept running the ultrasound wand over this one part of my breast, I know something is there, she was trying to capture it. After she left the room I looked at the screen and way at the bottom there were little thumbnails of each shot of my breast and I could tell some of them had neon orange spots and I imagined that that was where the computer had detected *cancer*. But I was too afraid to click around. I realize my hair looks so crazy and I'm naked and I quickly summon my dignity and leave.

Dashiell actually forgot they had to work at the preschool this afternoon, can you believe it. I actually can

believe it; they are sort of forgetful. Maybe it's the vitamin B deficiency or else that they sleep terribly every night, or adolescent weed-smoking or a traumatic childhood, we're not sure. I feel so bad that they have to go to work at the school feeling *freaked-out*, which they acknowledge they are feeling. When I climb out of the shower they are gone.

I go to the café where everyone is working on their screenplays and I get a bagel and cream cheese and a coffee and read Alexander Chee's *How to Write an Autobiographical Novel*. I walk to the thrift store down the street, texting my friend and my sister and my AA sponsee about my mammogram problem. My sister calls me right away. She is a hypochondriac and great in situations of other people's potential medical issues. She goes on Komen.org and assures me it's likely nothing and that breast cancer, unlike dense breasts, does not run in our family. And I breastfed. She feels too bad for me to let me off the phone but I eventually need the soothing environment of the thrift store, which is run by a sect of young Christians who are very sweet even though I always want to hold a grudge against a Christian, for the obvious reasons. I buy an interesting gold necklace and a pair of enamel earrings and for my son I find a Captain America shield that doubles as a *purse*, if you can believe it, then buy five kids' books so I can get the 50 percent–off discount: *Pinocchio* (Disney version), an Eric Carle book about a hermit crab, a lift-the-flap 1980s book about the human body, a story about an elephant who goes to Venice, Italy, because we are going to Venice, Italy, in May, and then a book about a little bunny that won't stop saying, "Poop-di-doop!," which I think my son will love because he himself cannot stop saying "poop" and "poopoohead" and "kill" and "die" and "dead" and "hate" and "pee."

At the preschool my spouse looks so weary running around cleaning every-thing up and I watch my son go down the slide a bunch, each time landing on his feet in a sort of pose, and I heap much praise upon him, though his friend Maisie actually lands on her feet and seamlessly transitions into a somersault and that is the real winner.

In the car I sit in the backseat with him and read the elephant book, which is sort of weird and boring and keeps talking about how great Diet Coke is, and then the poop-di-doop book, which, as I guessed, he loves. They drop me off at the café because I still have to work, the submission to that HBO script workshop is still due today, my emails are still languishing in my inbox, and so I go inside and set up my computer and get my new thing, a double espresso and a huge bottle of Topo Chico: it's caffeinating and also refreshing. And while I am working my phone rings and it's a Los Angeles number so I pick up in case it's my manager, and it's Betty from my doctor's office. Dashiell loves Betty. Dashiell has that vibe where they can charm older ladies and through the injecting of many vitamin B shots they have come to love each other, and Betty tells me my ultrasound is normal. I didn't expect to hear anything today. I run out of the café with my phone even though everyone is always loudly making deals on theirs in this café, I run out and stop myself from telling Betty all about my day. I text Dashiell and

I text my sister and my friend and my AA sponsee. I feel so good and we all go out and eat Mexican food for dinner and after dinner, when our son is asleep, I make a small batch of really weird cookies. I thought we were out of chocolate chips so I put in cocoa and cinnamon and then Dashiell found the chips and I put all of them in, too many, and it was Earth Balance instead of butter and maybe the recipe was bad, the sugar-to-flour ratio was off, but we eat them anyway and guzzle milk and watch *The Chilling Adventures of Sabrina* and Dashiell lies down because their back hurts and I put a pillow on their butt and put my head there and they sort of pet my head while I sort of pet the cat so he doesn't get jealous. And we watch TV and then we go to sleep.

Thankfully,

MICHELLE TEA
LOS ANGELES, CA

DEAR McSWEENEY'S,
It was 2001 when I, definitively and exhaustively, stopped thinking of things as "bad" or "good." Everyone got upset.

In 2008, about a week after giving birth to my older daughter, I did a reading with a Famous Male Author, quietly oozing milk and blood as I stood in front of a packed room, squeezing my thighs together and keeping my voice casual. It was very important for me to appear casual in front of all those people, in front of the male author, in front of my own inward gaze. I wish I'd let myself be as torn up as I felt; I wish I'd not participated in our cultural insistence on retouching childbirth into a breezy, everyday event, even if it does, in fact, happen every day. It happens every day, just like war and murder. Just because an occurrence is common doesn't mean it's not gory. One minute my body was turned inside out and the next minute I was sitting in a folding chair doing the head-tilt of reverence and absorption while my ears rang with ghostly cries of baby hunger and my heavily padded bra went fully damp. My girdled flesh rolled and stuck together, and pain occupied my lower half stolidly. The Famous Male Author read for forty-five minutes with the poise and confidence of someone who's never once been interrupted, let alone bled through a pair of pants.

The year 2009 heralded intrusive thoughts about both my infant daughter and my dissertation, about how to be less careful in my writing while being eminently careful with the fruit of my flesh, this serious creature who was of me but not me. I probed myself for how to be the best and smartest and most loving person I could be, probed and probed, until two soft spots formed above where my vena cava is. If I press down there even now, it hurts, as though a toothless vampire had gummed the flesh just so, repeatedly. I am my own toothless vampire. BE YOUR OWN TOOTHLESS VAMPIRE would look nice embroidered on a pillow, I think.

You can't think of things as "bad" or "good" unless you want to position yourself antagonistically against the world, unless you want to believe in sides, unless you are four years old, unless you are Donald Trump. I would never make it as a politician, because I'd be holding everything up to the light, bills and propositions and the nuclear football, and asking, *How does this make me feel, how does this*

make me grow, what can this teach me, where does this move me to go? My cabinet would be like, *Um, Madame President, workers are striking in Pensacola and a new encroaching terrorist cell has been uncovered in Montreal*, and I would be like, *Well, we need to consider all angles, all 9,875,156 angles. This could take some time. Let's call our mothers and our grandmothers and see what they think too. Let's commune with the dead.*

Everyone's always like, "You *pray?* Why on *earth?*" Listen, I have the *most stamina for talking* of anyone I've ever met, anyone you've ever met. What am I supposed to do when everyone falls asleep? Do you know what it's like to be the last person awake at the sleepover, decades after the sleepover has ended? I no longer call it insomnia; I call it my tundra of wakefulness. It's where I reprocess every bit of information I've ever been given, until it emerges—not bad, not good, just different from when it went in. You can call this information reprocessing unit a psyche or an existential fermentation plant, but I call it God.

Yours,

KRISTEN ISKANDRIAN
BIRMINGHAM, AL

DEAR McSWEENEY'S,

I got into a huge fight at the food court at Grand Central Terminal on Thanksgiving. Basically, a cashier tried to gaslight me into believing a poppy seed bagel was an everything bagel.

I usually go to my parents' house in New Jersey for Thanksgiving. The past couple years, though, my brother and his wife have been doing Thanksgiving Day with her family, and my sisters have stopped coming altogether, so my aunt invited my parents and me to her Thanksgiving in Connecticut.

Grand Central Terminal, where you catch a train to Connecticut, is a giant marble palace built by Cornelius Vanderbilt, with carved fountains and statues of cherubs and celestial paintings on the ceiling. Penn Station, where you catch the train to New Jersey and Long Island, on the other hand, is a one-block soft-pretzel store that doubles as a public restroom, and is much more hospitable to the homeless. I love it. New Jersey Transit operates out of the first floor, and Long Island Rail Road operates out of the basement (where, rumor has

it, they make Long Island commuters shovel coal into a big furnace to power the whole place).

A toasted bagel with butter is one of my favorite meals. It's warm, filling, and, depending on where you are, it costs between one and three dollars. I especially like poppy seed bagels, because I erroneously think they have a calming effect since poppy seeds come from opium plants. So I stood in line at a to-go counter in the basement of Grand Central on my way to my aunt's house and ordered a poppy seed bagel, toasted, with butter.

"We don't *have* poppy seed bagels," the cashier said.

I looked at a bowl on the counter with several poppy seed bagels in it and looked back at him. "Are you... sure?" I said.

"*Yeah.*"

"I'm sorry, I think that's a poppy seed bagel." I pointed to the poppy seed bagel.

"*No.* We don't *have* poppy seed bagels."

"Then what's that?"

"That's an *everything* bagel."

This went on for an astonishing amount of time. I felt like a crazy person, having to audibly say things like "But sir. If it was an everything bagel, it would have other things on it. Like garlic. Or other kinds of seeds." I stood my ground, and was very brave.

Eventually he called over his manager and told him to tell me they didn't have poppy seed bagels. The manager looked at the bowl and gave me a poppy seed bagel.

It tasted okay.

Thanksgiving with my cousins and all their extended family later that night was exciting. For one thing, their nana was there. Both of my grandmas are Irish, but this nana is *real* Irish, with a brogue and everything. Everyone was asking her what it was like growing up in Ireland and moving to the Bronx as a young person.

"Mom hated the movie *Brooklyn*," said one of the aunts who is not my aunt. "She said it was too realistic."

"It was so sad seeing my life up there. Moving to this place that isn't your home. So lonely. Who wants to see that?" said Nana.

"I like Saoirse Ronan," I said.

My aunt Mary, my dad's sister, told us about how traumatized she was from going to Ireland every summer as a child, where my grandma would send her to keep my great-grand-mother company.

"I had to leave civilization to go stay in this strange house in the middle of nowhere. They didn't have *any-thing* back then. If I wanted to drink anything other than water, I had to go milk an animal. When I had to pee in the middle of the night, I had to go out in the dark to an outhouse. I wasn't allowed to go anywhere unless your dad came with me."

My cousins rolled their eyes, hearing this story for the millionth time, but it was news to me.

"You never told us you went to Ireland every summer!" I said to my dad. "That's so weird! This sounds... significant!"

"Yeah. I dunno. I guess your aunt just remembers it better because she was younger."

A month later, at my nuclear fam-ily's Christmas dinner in New Jersey, my siblings and I were giggling about some militantly anti-English thing one of my uncles had said the night before at the annual Houlihan

Christmas Eve party. I laughed and said I didn't understand why someone who was born and raised in the US so vehemently identified as Irish.

"Well, it's probably because of that time he got beat up," said my brother. He relayed to us a secondhand story about how our uncle Jack got the shit beat out of him by some British Loyalist officers on a visit to Ireland when he was in his early twenties. His uncle Buddy, a priest, heard yelling outside his window, saw the scene, and ran out with their American passports to beg them to leave him alone.

"Yeah, it was crazy back then," my dad said. "Mom and I went there in 1981. We rented a car and were driving around—"

"Which was so weird!" my mom said. "The first time I went to Ireland, no one even *had* cars!"

So they were driving a rental car around Tyrone, where my mom's family is from. They parked in front of a post office, got out, and made it maybe fifty feet before a group of British soldiers ran over to them, carrying machine guns.

"What are you doing here?"

"We're sightseeing. We're tourists."

Nothing about this area looked to them like it was dangerous or required such high security. And my parents didn't look particularly suspicious.

"Sightseeing?"

My dad was confused about what the right answer was. "We're visiting from the United States."

"Give us your identification." My parents handed over their passports, proving they were American.

"Why is your car parked there?"

"The spot was open. We just want to walk around the neighborhood."

The soldiers walked my parents back to the car with their machine guns.

"Open the boot."

My dad was confused.

"The boot!"

"What's a boot?"

"Open the boot!" He walked my dad to the back of the car and pointed his gun at the trunk of the car.

"Oh, sure."

It seemed weird to my parents that the soldiers were so suspicious of them. My parents both have Bronx accents, not unlike Bugs Bunny or Tweety Bird (*I sawr a movie*; *I drank a cawfee*; et cetera). It's very unlikely that they could have been mistaken for Irish citizens, especially after showing their US passports.

My dad opened the trunk—boot—of the car and the soldier poked his gun around.

"Start the car."

My dad got into the front seat of the car and turned his key in the ignition. The engine hummed. He looked up at the soldier.

"What's the matter with you two? You're Americans just *randomly* leaving your car outside a government building?"

My parents realized: *the soldiers thought they were trying to blow up the post office.* They thought the car had a bomb in it and that it would detonate when my dad turned the key. Back home, why *wouldn't* you park a car in front of a post office? It'd be no different from parking it in front of a house or a vacant lot or a pizza place or a bank or an empty field or anywhere else.

The soldiers were through with them and left.

My siblings and I were amazed by this story, particularly picturing my dad getting bullied with machine guns. While we were on the subject of scary Ireland stories, I asked my mom: "Didn't your grandma have a boyfriend right before she moved here who was shot to death by British soldiers? And, like, a bridge was named after him or something?"

She looked at me like I was crazy.

"No."

"Oh."

"It was her *cousin.* He was *beaten* to death by some Black and Tans, but they *had* guns. And the bridge isn't *named* after him; it's just *engraved* with his name."

I don't think that's very different from what I said.

Anyway, I should probably be going.

Thanks for listening,

MARY HOULIHAN
BROOKLYN, NY

ONLY THE LONELY

by JINCY WILLETT

IN 1957, BETTY'S MOTHER told her that if anyone ever broke into the house when she was by herself, and she couldn't escape, she should act insane. "It might confuse him," she said, "and while he's trying to figure you out, you can run around screaming." Now it was 2018, and Betty was a seventy-one-year-old orphan with bad knees, barely able to escape from her bed in the morning. And here, finally, was her intruder, outlined in moonlight at the foot of her bed.

For a minute she tried to convince herself that this was a hypnagogic hallucination, like the twinkling, airborne spiders that often confronted her when she woke in the dark. She had learned to wait these out. She tried to wait out the intruder, who only came into sharper focus.

This was bad. She did not *feel* it was bad—she simply knew it. As she lay waiting to feel it, she began to tease out some of his facial features—the moonlight threw shadows onto his nose and right cheek, so she could see that his face was plump and round. Either he was wearing a hoodie that flopped over his forehead or he had bangs. He looked like Roy Orbison. This meant he wasn't wearing a mask, unless it was a mask of Roy Orbison.

Betty had watched enough true-crime reenactments to know that you maybe had a shot if they didn't think you could recognize them. But here was his actual face. She was going to die—soon, if she was lucky.

He still didn't move. Did he see that her eyes were open? Was he waiting for some reaction? Was she supposed to scream now? Whenever she tried to scream in dreams, nothing came out but mewling. Anyway, her neighbors wouldn't hear, because the bedroom window was shut. Screaming was probably what he wanted. Her scream was the first line in his fantasy. Betty knew this, just as she knew that his fantasy was trite. She was going to die a bit actor in a foolish play.

Now she realized that she was waiting not for Roy Orbison but for the fear, which began to shimmer in the farthest reaches of her mind. But there was time now, while it shimmered, to make a choice or two. Was she paralyzed? Let's find out, she thought, reaching for the bedside lamp, turning it on, sitting up straight, smiling at Roy Orbison. "There you are!" she said.

Roy Orbison blinked and stepped back. He held something in his left hand. A gun? A knife? Betty decided not to look.

"I'd just about given up on you!" Betty flung the covers aside and got out of bed, slipping on her sandals. Without looking to her right, she grabbed her bathrobe and pulled it on, knotting it at the waist. She took a second to admire her old black-watch Pendleton robe. Her room, the part not occupied by Roy Orbison, was neat, orderly, warm in the LED light. A decent place to die. Unless some idiot knocked things over and messed it up with blood. She turned to look at him, making her expression cheerful, though not too cheerful. "Are you hungry?" she asked. What if he was a cannibal? "I have eggs," she said. "Would you like French toast?"

Long silence. "Yeah?"

His voice was hoarse, pitched mid-range. He wasn't exactly looking at her now. He was looking inward, thinking. Thinking was hard.

Beckoning him to follow, she walked out of the bedroom into the kitchen; she could hear him shuffling behind her, and the fear shimmered closer. In the kitchen she pulled out a chair for him, resolving to face him from now on, whatever happened. Turning her back was not a good idea. How would she make French toast and stay facing him? She got out eggs, bread, and butter, and turned the gas on under the skillet. As she worked, she kept glancing at him. He watched her incuriously, as though she were passing scenery viewed from a bus window. His left hand, holding whatever it was, remained in his lap.

Betty loaded up his plate and set it before him. "Syrup?" she asked. "I have maple."

"Yeah."

She handed him a fork and a bottle of syrup. She was damned if she was going to pour it for him.

It was a knife, not a gun. He was left-handed: he set it down beside the plate, picked up the fork, and started to eat. Not an eating knife. The black handle had three curves in it for gripping, and the blade was short with a wide, nasty beveled edge. Some sort of hunting tool. He didn't look fit enough to be a hunter. A cellar dweller with a fish-belly complexion, he chewed with his mouth open. She was going to be butchered by a greedy, petulant dolt.

She opened the kitchen drawer beside the stove. In it were a meat tenderizer, a potato peeler, a lemon zester, a melon baller, an egg slicer, and an ancient Ginsu knife, a perfect weapon if you're being menaced by a loaf of bread. The other side of the kitchen, behind Roy Orbison, was where she kept screwdrivers, wrenches, and a ball-peen hammer. She briefly considered chancing a glide past him to the drawer; he seemed wholly engaged with his plate. She imagined lifting the hammer high, bringing it down with all her strength (which wasn't much, except you were supposed to be unnaturally strong in certain adrenaline-fueled situations), feeling it sink into the back of his skull. Could she do that? Not at the moment. She wasn't frightened enough.

She wasn't frightened at all.

Maybe she should let the fear in. It was back there, tapping its foot.

"Tell me all about yourself," she said, sitting down across from him.

Nothing but slurping, lip-smacking, heavy breathing through a clogged nose. Betty, who had once been a syndicated advice columnist, recalled a letter-writer whining on about her crippling, marriage-dooming misophonia. Way too late, she empathized with Nauseous in Nashville, who must be long dead. How had she died? Not like this.

"I asked you a question," she said.

He looked up, startled. Syrup drooled from the corner of his chapped mouth.

"For example," she said, "what is your name?"

He started to answer, thought better of it, scowled at her, meeting her eyes for the first time. "I'm gonna kill you," he said. Had his voice not risen at the end like a guess, this might have been scary.

"Of course you are."

"Gonna slice you open, you bitch." Not a guess. He was trying to work himself up to the moment.

"Well, good for you!" Her voice was much louder than his. She assaulted him with a wide smile. She showed him all her teeth.

"I'm gonna gut you like a floon!" he shouted, blushing suddenly, like a camouflaging octopus. "A fish! Gonna glut you like a fish!"

Betty laughed.

Now he grabbed the knife. Was this what she had been trying to get him to do? Why? To make him bring on the fear? And why do that? It wasn't working, anyway.

She stood, bent forward, looming over him, arching her throat right in front of him, flaunting it. "Glut me like a fish, you crazy, beautiful nut!" she cried. "Gut me like a floon! Flut me like a goon!" These would be her last words.

Oh, why the hell not. Who said she had to cry and scream and snivel for her life? Where was it written that her job was to put herself inside this wretched head?

Roy Orbison sliced the blade across her beloved Pendleton, exposing the purple flowers of her nightgown.

Here, finally, we go, and the fear galloped in, inches behind her. Okay, right there was exactly where she needed it; she would let it breathe down her neck, stay just ahead of it. Betty didn't exactly have a plan, but she did have a clear goal: to make the rest of Roy Orbison's inner life a living hell.

"All my life I've had this recurring dream about you," she lied, her voice low and husky, "and now here you are. It's a holy miracle." Her recurring dream was about furious women throwing tarantulas at her bare feet, but he didn't need to know that.

"Shut up."

"*You* shut up!"

"Bitch!"

"Same face, same jacket, same knife. All these years I've been waiting for this exact moment! Swear to god!"

"Bullcrap!"

"Bullcrap! Ha ha! I knew you were going to say that!"

"Yeah, well, you're not going to be laughing in a minute!" He stood up, pushing the table back into her. "I know what you're doing," he said.

"Of course you do!"

"You're stalling for time!"

"Can you blame me, you glorious lunatic?"

Still keeping the table between them, he motioned toward the hallway door. "Get back there!" He was beginning to achieve a rhythm, regain his footing. She imagined the gears in his head waggling, working to re-mesh.

"Why? Do you have laundry?"

"I will *kill you!*" He sliced the robe again, this time vertically. *Bastard.* Betty loved that robe.

"There's really no need to shout," she said, her voice lower, scolding him like a fond nanny, and then, because he was finally advancing around the table toward her, she threw up her hands in mock surrender. "I just want to know where we're going. Laundry… or bath?"

"The fucking bathroom!"

"Language," said Betty, backing down the hall, pausing at the bathroom door. "Go right ahead, dear," she said. "I'll wait."

He pushed her inside, not hard enough to make her lose her footing. He reached into his right pocket, fished out a necktie, and threw it to her. "Tie yourself to that pipe."

"Was this your dad's?" Betty examined the ugly thing, one of those '70s clown ties; it smelled like pizza. "Do you always use it, or do you have a perfect one for each occasion?"

"Never mind. Do what I said."

"Not until you tell me your name."

He slapped her across the face with the hand that wasn't holding the knife. The slap wasn't much, but it was still a shock. Their first intimacy.

It was also a slap to the face, and without a thought she slapped him back, much harder, knocking him against the sink, surprising them both. In the time it took him to right himself, she considered and rejected flight strategies. She probably couldn't outrun him; besides, flight would be undignified. Then again, so would strangulation, evisceration, violation, dismemberment, whatever else he had in his tiny mind. But that would be later; this was now. Now was hers. She stood still.

"Look," she said, "there's something you need to understand. I have arthritis. I can't tie myself to anything, including that pipe, which I can't reach anyway. See?"

He pressed up against her, holding the blade of the knife to her throat.

"Clearly you have plans, but if you don't tell me what they are, I can't help you with them."

He opened his mouth and panted. He was trembling.

"Everything is possible," she said, "but there are steps. There are protocols." She reached around with both hands and cupped his head, bringing him close, nose to nose, whispering. "We need to talk."

"I hate you," he said. "I hate you so much."

Betty kissed him. She hadn't kissed a man in forty years—no, thirty-five, because there was that King Features assclown she'd run into at that dumb Toledo conference, and what a screw-up that had been. "I'm divorced, Tiger," she had told him. "I've closed up shop," and then they had hit the bar. Roy Orbison's lips felt and tasted disgusting, but no more so than Mel Wanamaker's had.

He pushed her away and wiped his mouth.

She stared at him, hard, and wiped her own mouth slowly with the back of her hand, mirroring him exactly. "If you find kissing me so repulsive," she said, "you might ask yourself what you're doing here."

"What I'm doing here is killing you."

"You and heartburn and Trump and my damn arthritis. You're all killing me. Killing me doesn't make you special, Roy."

For the first time, he relaxed, a little, and smiled. "But the way I do it," he said.

"Ah."

"Takes a loooong time."

"Are you going to bore me to death?"

"Keep it up. Just keep it up! Every stupid thing you say will make it even worse. You'll beg me—"

"Wait! Don't tell me! I'll beg you to end my suffering?"

"You'll beg me, you'll promise to do anything, *anything*, if I just won't kill you, if I just stop—"

"I'm confused. You couldn't stand me kissing you, so why would I try to entice you with sexual whoopee?"

"It's not—" He started to pant again. "I don't want—"

"What you want," she said, soothingly, "is to *humiliate* me. Right?"

"Yeah!" For a confused moment, he looked grateful, then that tiny burst of fellow-feeling knocked him back.

"Sorry, Tiger. When you reach a certain age…" Was this true? Did age make you humiliation-proof? She flashed on the third-grade play, when she had last-minute improvised a bridal veil by fastening a half-slip to her head and Mrs. Votolato had run onstage and snatched it off. She was eight years old and this was the final time she'd cried in public. What could Roy Orbison do to eclipse the ignominy of "Mr. Toad's Wild Wedding"? Zilch, because she and Roy were in a *private* place, not out there for the world to see. "You could learn a lot," she said, "from Mrs. Votolato."

He stared at her.

"Can't you see her?"

"You trying to be funny?"

Betty pointed at the wicker clothes hamper. "There she is. Face like a barn owl, built like a hydrant, Speedy Gonzales in her Red Cross shoes. She made us memorize bad poems. You want to torture somebody? Start with her."

Roy studied his knife, really studied it, as though there were a message on it.

"Be like the bird, who, halting in its flight on limb too slight, feels it give way beneath him—yet sings, knowing he hath wings!"

He took a tentative step toward her.

"Behind him lay the gray Azores! Behind the gates of Hercules—"

"It's not working," he whispered, trying to believe that.

"Be good, sweet maid, and let who will be clever—"

He lunged, sweeping the knife back and forth as though the room were pitch-dark and he were doing his best to defend himself, and she had just enough time to grab the plunger and bat the knife out of his hand, but she was wedged against the toilet and there was no room to get around him. He hesitated, trying to decide whether to lay weaponless hands on her actual body or bend down for the knife, and she fumbled blindly behind her back, came up with a can of air freshener, and sprayed him in the face with Glade.

"You old bitch!" He screamed and clawed at his eyes. What a child. It wasn't acid, for god's sake; it was Pumpkin Pit Stop Limited Edition, and why was she standing there staring at the can? Well, because it had words on it, and she pushed him over onto his back and retrieved the knife.

And now she was stuck. Roy Orbison wriggled like a pill bug on the bathroom tile, but if she ran out to get to the phone, he might get back up. She'd have to deal with him here and now, and *she had a knife in her hand.*

In the seconds it took him to uncurl and start to rise, she tried to imagine cutting into him and knew this was not possible quite yet; she couldn't do it if she deliberated about it first; she would need to be acting on pure instinct, and her husband had been so right: she overthought everything, put it all into words—herself, their marriage, their lives together—analyzed it all away, and no wonder he left. Nothing ever gets to you, he'd said. Not even me. But look, I actually slapped this guy, she thought, and I did spray him in the face; I didn't think first, and wasn't that a start? She wished he were there. Not to help, but to see.

Roy Orbison grabbed her left ankle and she sliced into the back of his hand clear to the bone, and the gross red streak across his knuckles shocked them both. "Look!" he screamed. He cradled the hand against his chest, rocking from side to side.

Ignoring a mad impulse to apologize, she grabbed the clown tie from the toilet tank and threw it down to him. "Tie *your* hands together," she said.

"I'm bleeding!"

"Everybody bleeds, Roy."

"Why do you keep calling me that?"

"Just do it!"

"Fuck you!"

Betty brandished the knife in front of his face, pointing it down toward his eyes. She had no idea if she could use it again. He stared, not at the knife, but at her. They both held their breath. What did he see in her face? She would have given a lot to know.

Roy Orbison closed his eyes, sighed, slumped back.

"Tie your hands. Do it."

He made a hash of it, wrapping the tie around each wrist, holding each end in his teeth, and ending up with what looked like a double shoelace bow. Clearly, that alone wouldn't hold him, and there were no ropes, let alone handcuffs, in the bathroom. In despair, she glanced around, looking for something, anything, that would immobilize him, but there was only a pair of gray sweatpants folded on top of the hamper. She bent down and tried wrapping the pant legs around his torso, but he wouldn't stop writhing or shut up; he kept threatening her life and whining about his burning eyes and his bleeding hand, and in the end she pulled the pants over his head and tied them around his neck with the drawstring. Now he was blind and would remain so for a while, maybe, and there were no blueprints for this.

On TV a woman in her situation would behave in time-honored ways. Would run for the door on feet much fleeter than her own, would stumble and sprawl and be grabbed or would make it outside to safety, would snag a phone and dial 911 or find that its wire was cut, would locate a weapon and use it, either brutally or ineptly. In one version would be table-turning savagery and blood and brains and screaming; in the other a pathetic glancing blow and the monster grabbing the weapon and turning it on her, and blood and brains and screaming.

But right now there was very little blood and not even that much disarray, and she still did not have a scream in her. Still.

She sat down on the toilet and just watched him. The knot was loosening, and she considered tightening it, but he wasn't even trying to free his hands. Maybe he was just depressed. He crawled about, rubbing his swaddled head against the wall and the sides of the tub, unable to work up enough friction to loosen the grip of her sweatpants. He looked like a huge, faceless lop-eared rabbit. He was muttering obscenities, but to himself. He did not realize she was still there, or he didn't care.

"You've never done this before, have you?"

His head jerked and banged against the tub.

"What's your name?"

He sighed. "Why?" he finally said. "Why is that such a deal to you?"

"Just wondered," she said. That wasn't true. She needed to know his name.

"Carl Proulx."

"With an *lx*?"

"Yeah, with an *lx*. What is your fucking deal?"

"You look like Roy Orbison."

"I don't know who that is."

The long silence that followed wasn't exactly companionable, but it wasn't uncomfortable either. She was going to have to call 911. Right now that seemed more an embarrassing chore than anything else; she was bone-tired and out of sorts.

There was a line of sight between the hall phone and the bathroom. "I can see you," she said, rising painfully, her knees rusted. "Move and I'll be back."

He said nothing.

"I'm calling the police now."

"Go nuts."

Betty had never dialed 911 in her life. As she did so, she kept an eye on the pathetic figure slumped against her bathroom wall. "I have," she cleared her throat, "I have an intruder. My address is—"

"911. What is your emergency?"

"As I said, there's an intruder. I've tied him up and—"

"Is there an active shooter?"

"No! An intruder. He just had a knife and—"

"Ma'am, is anybody injured?"

"Not really. Listen, I just need—"

"Ma'am, stay calm. An ambulance is on its way."

"Ambulance? Don't you want my address? I need the police—"

"You're at 1920 Stonybrook Court. Are you able to open the door?"

"Well, of course I know how to open the goddamn door. I just want—"

"Don't panic, ma'am. Help is—"

Betty slammed down the phone, which rang again immediately. She just set it down on the table and let the woman drone on. She opened the front door so they wouldn't bash it in, then went back to the bathroom and sat with Carl Proulx. "That woman," she told him, "is an idiot." Together they waited.

There were lights and thundering hooves and a lot of "ma'am"s. She had to tell the police four times, from beginning to end, what had happened and why Carl Proulx was tied up and injured. It didn't help that she kept forgetting and calling him Roy Orbison. To placate them she did her best to give them what they wanted, a dotty old bag addled out of her wits by the terrifying events of the night. Yes, she said, she had been badly frightened, but she was better now, and no, she did not want to go to the hospital, and thanks, but she didn't need to call anyone to stay with her. They would have forced some sort of aid upon her if she hadn't assured them that her daughter Rose was on her way. Both her daughters lived in New Mexico, and she hadn't spoken to them, or wanted to, for ten years. *Get the hell out of my house*, she'd refrained from saying. Eventually they had.

They cuffed Carl Proulx and led him stumbling down her front walk. Somebody had slid the sweatpants up off his face to check him out, but now they'd slipped back down. "For god's sake," she called after them, "take those pants off his head; the man can't see a thing."

She locked down and straightened up the house. He hadn't made much of a mess, not really. Her robe was ruined, but the blood smears on the tiles and tub were easy to wipe clean, and her bedroom seemed untouched, as though he had never stood there (for how long?) at the foot of her bed. There were no footprints on the hardwood floor.

For the first time she wondered how he'd gotten in. The back door was latched; no windows were open or unlocked, and she clearly remembered unlocking the front door to let in the police. Had he gotten in when she was out shopping for groceries? She'd been home by seven. He could, she supposed, have jimmied a door and locked up behind himself, but where had he waited? For at least six hours? Her house was small. She went from room to room, searching out evidence.

When she got to the guest room closet, she had already convinced herself she'd been wrong about the front door. The alternative was that he had materialized through the wall or, worse, that she had had some sort of brain event and imagined the night from beginning to end. Expecting nothing, she slid open the closet door, and there was his nest.

A big black flashlight, her Maglite, cadged from the pantry drawer. A bed of sorts fashioned from her summer clothes, pulled down from their hangers and layered neatly along the length of the closet. He'd bunched up her terry robe and beach towels for his pillow. The bed was littered with Cheeto crumbs, and on it lay a flattened, spine-cracked book. It was her own copy of Rebecca West's *The Meaning of Treason*, and he'd apparently made it to page 95. She leaned into the closet and inhaled. He must have done laundry today; her closet smelled like Cheetos and Febreze.

Betty made herself a drink. Before turning off the kitchen lights, she noticed the empty Cheetos bag in the wastebasket. Had he had time to pick up after himself and get back into the closet while she was out? No. He must have done this *after* she got home. Before he woke her. Maybe while she was bathing? Or after she fell asleep.

She downed the drink and then another, took a pill, brushed her hair, got into bed, turned out the light, and waited. At first for sleep, which didn't come, and then for Roy, who would never come again, and at last for the fear.

Surely now the fear would come for her. He had lain silent in her house, ten feet away, planning mayhem and murder. Aloud, in the dark, she asked, "How can I ever feel safe here?" Perhaps this would jump-start the fear. But of course it didn't, because it was theatrical, absurd; she had never been foolish enough to feel safe anywhere.

The fear had been real while he was here, and she had disrespected it, toyed with it, put it off, used it like a tool. But now she was ready. More than ready. Hungry. She did not know why, but she needed it. In the dark she waited for the fear, opened herself humbly, her first act of faith, and waited, and waited, but in the end there was only dawn.

IF WE COULD
STAY LIKE
THIS FOREVER

by GENEVIEVE HUDSON

GEORGE IS AN ARIES with an Aries rising and an Aries moon. And she isn't my girlfriend. She is my girl comma friend whom I live with and with whom I share bunk beds. She is better than a wife because she is forever. We would make a horrible romantic pair because I am a Cancer with a Cancer moon and a Cancer rising, and Cancers, those poor, crushable crustaceans, are the embodiment of two words and those words are *I feel*. George does not like to feel. I feel for her, which is something I can only do for a friend. I feel enough for the both of us and she thinks and burns for the both of us too.

George is beautiful. I mean, really, she is stunning in that are-you-a-model kind of way. Her neck is extraordinarily long. Her upturned nose sits in the middle of a perfectly square face. That jawline, though. Someone could write a dissertation about its symmetry. Its angles. I'm waiting to find it on JSTOR. It's coming. George has broken the soul of many an academic, and writing is the best form of catharsis.

It is sometimes difficult for George, because she is so pretty that people are routinely mean to her. Especially in the city we live in, which is progressive and against makeup, and where the more tattoos you have, the more you are rewarded with social tokens like free coffee. For this reason, I think it is brave that George continues to frequent the tanning salon, to forgo the color black most days of the week, to remain without a single piercing on her face. She even refuses to get a tiny drawing of a household object tattooed onto her arm. She maintains her appearance by driving out to the Sephora in the suburbs because the coconut oil–based makeup they sell in the city boutiques washes away in the rain. I don't mind that most people mistake George for my girlfriend. We play into it, bring identical lunches to the bookstore where we work, and sit in the break room eating our dairy-free protein bars, containers of kale salad, carrot sticks, and packets of raw nut butters while calling each other Wife.

George is not one for affection, but when she is feeling tender and open to emotional connection, she'll look at me from her armchair across the room, where she'll be cutting out pictures of natural disasters, nasal her voice into something that does not sound like it would come from her, and say, "Snuggling!"

Then I will say, "Snuggling!"

We do not touch. We say the words and that is enough.

Afterward, we eat bowls of frozen grapes with almond milk drizzled over them, talk about the afterlife, drink big mugs of magnesium citrate, fall fast asleep in our bunk beds feeling like the world is smaller than we could ever have imagined.

*　　*　　*

We've been living together for years before we get the idea for *If We Could Stay Like This Forever*. Or, I get the idea. We're still obsessed with death. Of course we are. We see it crouched behind the surface of every moment, waiting. We love to wind each other up with Fear Talk.

"Careful when you walk to your car. Sometimes men hide under there with razor blades, slash your ankles, and pull you into the backseat for raping."

"Watch out for black ice on the bridge. You'll likely careen off the side into the churn of dark water."

We Fear Talk with a religious intensity until my IBS comes back, and George eats all the nails off her hands so that wearing Band-Aids on each finger becomes necessary.

On the same night that a plane disappears over the Pacific Ocean, George's father calls to tell her about an opportunity at his friend's gallery. An opening, and are we interested?

"Is that like *wink, wink, come up with something and you're in?*" I ask.

George's father is a prominent Hollywood director, and George played the baby in a famous movie from the '80s. You've definitely seen it. Everyone has. George wants to be an artist just like her dad, live a creative life, never work a nine-to-five, walk into a room and cause strangers to whisper. She thinks of herself as visually astute, and I don't disagree. I was trained as a visual artist, but the only thing I have to show for it is a mound of student debt and a group show in the attic of my alma mater's arts building that I called *Faces* because I drew a lot of faces for the occasion.

George clutches her phone to her heart and says, "We're going to be a star."

Her father is ninety-seven, so we are running out of time to take advantage of his big connections. I feel a sense of urgency spill into me. George pirouettes around the living room, shows off her early ballet training. She waltzes in front of the TV like she doesn't need a partner to lead. She holds one of her boxes and waltzes with it.

George is obsessed with boxes. She could make them all day long. She makes boxes from glass and cardboard. That's her art. She stacks them in precarious shapes and photographs them against white walls. Boxes to stack on boxes. Delicate boxes. Unbreakable boxes. So many boxes.

Fuck boxes, I think.

Her idea for our exhibition is to build large-scale boxes made of mirrors that she will source from a factory in Boring, Oregon. She tells me I can help her assemble the boxes. A partnership. Kind of. She suggests we call the show *Boxes*.

I hold up my hand.

I say, "No," and I mean it.

On the television behind George, CNN reports on the plane that has disappeared. Air traffic control lost contact with the plane hours ago, and hope of finding it has diminished to zero. Now, that is art. The lost plane flies through my third eye. It plunges into the ink of my subconscious. I can't stop picturing the rows of bodies in various states of wakefulness, the movies playing in the backs of seats, the music filling their ears. When did the passengers know their lives would end? What did they do in their final moments? How long did it last? I remember myself in a flight with much turbulence, a plane that did not go down. I remember the book in my lap. The girlfriend next to me, whom I could have died with, whom I could have bathed in those final moments with. She would have become the most important person in my life, because she would have left life with me. We would have been each other's last girlfriends. It's true that where you end is more important than anything in the middle.

I tilt my chin toward George, still engaged in her box waltz, and in the same voice we use to tell each other we are "snuggling," I say, "Not boxes, George. Not boxes. No more boxes."

I point to our origami swan, the one she made from a napkin on the night we met. Our paper angel. It's staring at us from the wall where I pinned it with a single nail. It's telling us that something is going to happen.

Death had come close to both of us before, its black robe billowing behind, to snuff out my dad's dog, my neighbor's cat, my kid brother whose blood was bad. But death didn't dare touch me. My young-girl biceps grew to the size of oranges from punching flour bags that hung from the rafters of my parents' garage. My strength made me dangerous, death-proof. Punch. The bag swung out and back. Knuckle to canvas. Nothing would mess with me or I'd come swinging. Grim was the way my mouth felt, a line drawn across my lower face. My thighs loved it when I took them on a run. Ligament and bone and tendon. One look at me and you'd see I'd taste terrible. I would be all chew and sinew, a collagen afterglow. My body was a body for the world, not for death. Death! The world loved my body. I fed it swollen figs that would splat into sugar puddles on our back patio. In my hands, the bees swarmed the fat figs and fought me for the guts. Juice leaked from the splits in their sides and bled sugar. The bees swarmed my lips. They sat in my ears humming. I once swallowed four bees and they flew down my throat. I heard them buzzing in my belly for days. Then one morning they went silent, and I knew they were gone.

George's childhood was death-filled too. Her older brother walked off a high dive into a waterless pool on purpose. Both of us with dead brothers, a memory we share. Her mother left but didn't die and what's the difference. She put on paper wings and stepped into a station wagon. Gone is gone.

Her father stayed in his mansion. A king in his castle who called her toward him with her own queen-size bed, a private floor, a Porsche when she turned sixteen. She wandered the halls of the mansion, the gold-trimmed corridors like the gilded throat of a god. Her life might have seemed perfect if it had not been so lonely. Not even the maids wanted to braid her hair, because George was too beautiful to touch. Her posture was too perfect. Her smile was turned to just the right station. There is a distance in beauty. No one wants to get too close.

George and I fill our living room with images of the final moment before death. We will display such images at our installation. Finding the right ones is key. We spend entire weekends streaming YouTube videos of deadly crashes. We pause the films right before the impact. We tape pictures to our walls and to our ceiling until everything is covered in photographs of pre-disaster.

The person in the car is still unharmed.

The man crossing the street is fine.

The couple boarding the train is safe and sound.

The girls walking the bridge are happy because it has not collapsed. But it will. It will.

Cell phone footage of a train before it derails in the Austrian Alps.

A photo of a man perched on the windowsill of a tower while it burns.

An audio file of a woman realizing her parachute isn't going to open.

Still fine, but.

These images will spread across the bright white walls of a high-ceilinged gallery. The soundscape I assemble will play in the background: the mutters of the not-yet-dead. Their chorus will shift and flap like a crow batting through the rafters.

We stop going to work at the bookstore. Our manager calls and calls, but we are watching a surfer paddle into a wave, where he will be eaten by a shark. Soon the manager will stop calling, and we will not notice, because we will be listening to the sounds of a boy hiking at dusk before he comes face to face with an angry moose. We will watch these images until our eyes are dry and drained and rimmed in red. We can no longer walk through our house. It is too full of research. We are left to climb over the stacks of papers and photographs and step through beams of projected light. We stop changing our clothes and we lurk through the living room in loungewear, our gray suits of sweat material and socks of blended wool. We forget to eat, so immersed are we in our research, and when hunger hits we discover that the cabinets contain nothing but nut butter. So it is spoons overflowing with ground macadamias we consume and, in the end, it is enough. We milk its fat for our brains. I discover a tin of sardines under the sofa and we slurp them down while listening to the Bear Man, as he was known, get eaten by his bear friends. We do not blink, do not smile, do not frown. We listen. The fish we have devoured swim through us.

Scrolling through videos one night, I watch a boy on a curb in a city take the hand of an elder. They intend to cross the busy street together. A small, safe thing. But the street they will cross will be bombed because of war. These are the minutes just before. They don't know it, but I do.

What appears in the mind of the boy when he looks up and sees the object of fire approaching? Does he realize that when he opens his mouth to scream, the air on his teeth, the out-breath over tongue, it will be his final time? Maybe he simply feels his body beat with blood—the quickened pulse, the spun silk of his spit, the hairs that stand tall and attentive on the back of his neck, the arch of his obedient spine.

Staring at this image is safe, and the wrongness of that suddenly has weight.

I feel it. There is no urgency to what we are doing and nothing to risk. My loungewear is so comfy it is almost grotesque. The boy explodes on-screen, and I could fall asleep sitting up. That's how relaxed I am. Our project is padded in security. Is that art? Capital *N-O*, answers my mind quickly and with resolve.

"How can we capture a feeling we've never tried to understand?" asks George the Mind Reader from her perch on the couch.

George has paused the recording she was listening to, which a group of lost hikers left behind. The hikers, poor mortals, were stuck in the woods with the knowledge that snow would fall that night and freeze the life from them. They are saying goodbye, speaking into the fuzz hum of the recording device, and god do they sound alive. People have never sounded so vibrant, so healthy, so pure. They could not fall asleep even if they tried.

"What can we really know of these people's final moments while swaddled in such comfort? We are cheating. Are we cheaters? Is that who we want to be?"

"Do we have to die?" I ask.

"Maybe," says George, quick quiver on her lower lip.

If we are to fully inhabit other people's pre-death moments, we must harness our purest selves and polish our senses. George's acupuncturist instructs her to drink only water that has been steeped in rose quartz; to buy organic dish soap, place a dime of it on her Jupiter finger, and rub it into the middle of her forehead right over her third eye; to bathe in Epsom salts and coconut milk. This will heighten our perception and cleanse our inner knowings. For a while, it seems like these rituals will be enough. If we can elevate our senses, we can amplify our compassion. We might understand death without experiencing it. The suffering of someone else might be felt inside us firsthand.

We meditate for days. Fast on fruit vinegar. Dry-brush our skin until it bleeds. We become so sensitive that we cry when the other sneezes. The sight of a broken fingernail sends me into a spiral. Our empathy could bench-press the world. I develop fungus of the feet. George grows tinea versicolor on her shoulders. These are signs, we tell ourselves, that our bodies are shedding the bad. We are purifying. We are becoming one consciousness. We tape our mouths shut as we sleep to deepen our slumber. We pee the bed often.

One morning we are bathing in coconut milk and George is washing her hair with cedar oil. I love the smell of the coconut and salt mixing into a brine. It smells like an expanded mind. On the edge of the tub, we burn wood chips and dried herbs we bought at the magic store down the street, the one staffed by one young witch who talks so low we think she might be reciting a spell against us. Or for us. For us, we decide. Pasted to the walls of our bathroom are more final moments. Their edges curl from the bath steam. The moment that's missing is ours. We hardly talk to each other in English anymore but recite curious non-sentences, bleats and caws, that we construct from sound and innuendo and that we intuitively understand. But George speaks in English now, and I pay attention.

"We must enter the darkness firsthand," George says. "We must walk to the edge of death and take a look. Watching is no longer enough."

A thin yellow film coats her eyes. A milky scab is affixed to her chin. I hadn't noticed it until now, and when I blink, it's gone. Her face is as smooth as a hot-printed page.

George brings me to the edge of a twenty-story building, and we step onto the dizzying ledge. Our toes reach over into the air. We hold our breath and lean into the tipping point.

We slip stones into our pockets and walk into a dark lake. The stones are oblong pieces of world, palm-sized or smaller. I clutch them in my fist and pet them with my thumb. Their weight in our pockets is much. Death rocks that drive us down. They pull us earthward as we slog down the hill that descends into muck, submerged. I look up and see a sky wrinkled by the water we are under. Hello, sky, where inhalation is possible. My lungs burn. The burning is full and pressing. My eyes flash red, a sign of uh-oh. My fists are quick to empty out the stones, overturn my pockets, rush my mouth to the surface, where breath waits. Death did feel near. The reaper waited with her scythe.

But these things are too small and not enough.

At night in our bunk beds, George on top and me on the bottom, we construct the plan. She will rent the car, I the camera equipment. We will find a cliff to drive off. We will document our final moment, the moment before we die. We will speak into the recorder as George presses her foot against the gas, as the car lifts off the ground, when there's nothing under the tires but air.

We continue to practice meditation, heighten our awareness, and refine our senses into sharp pencils of precision. We need to extend the final moment to its absolute brink. We want to inhale each curve and dazzle of the death experience. We want to sink our teeth into the lips of our mortality. We want to feel death rush into the space between our toes and fill the gaps between the sickles of rib. We will become famous. Our performance will reveal itself on the front pages of every newspaper. People will flock to the gallery to see our show assembled, the one we will call *If We Could Stay Like This Forever*. Our final moment will last forever.

I remember the cold tiles of my childhood. Thistooshallpass. The pain is no more than a memory now, something I have reached the other side of. Death can be like that too.

It's sunny and bright on the morning we plan to drive our car off the cliff. The camera equipment is by the door, ready. We have not left the house in many weeks, except to go to the witch and magic store for rose oil. But on this day, George rises, applies her favorite lippy to her mouth like she hasn't done in ages, paints her nails hot pink, and pulls on her favorite gold onesie. She looks just like herself. Her hair droops taillike over one shoulder in a loose braid. She leaves to get the rental car, and I stand on our front porch. Torn pieces of cloud nap in the sky. A power line jitters and buzzes. I feel its electricity jacking me all the way up. My nose runs. I think I must have a fever. A family of pink-haired people passes by on the sidewalk. Across the block, three more women with pink hair pedal by on bicycles. I haven't felt the sun on my arms in ages. It slaps my skin. It pulls my capillaries to the surface, and they smile.

Before I know it, I'm walking toward the lesbian bar to get a beer. I don't care that it's only 10 a.m. As I walk, I feel the sun smacking me. The grass smells like grass. I'm not wearing shoes, so the pavement burns, and the pebbles press into the pads of my feet, but I don't care. This too shall pass. We could stay like this forever if we wanted. I swing open the door to the bar and it looks just like it always did, before I met George. Death is like that, too, I think. Death is a door I can walk through. When I inhale, the bacteria on my tongue tingles. I can taste the yeast of the place. I sit at a big brown table, and I squint into the dark. There is Margarita, walking across the unwashed floor, shaking her head like I'm crazy, like she's wondering where I've been. And I think I could sit here forever, not ever dying at all.

HOW A MAN CRUMBLES

by DANIIL KHARMS

—They say all fine gals are fat-arsed. But I—I go after the busty ones, I prefer their smell.

Having uttered this, he starts to increase in height and, upon reaching the ceiling, crumbles into a thousand tiny little balls. The street sweeper, Panteley, immediately arrives, sweeps all these balls into his bag with which he usually picks up horseshit, and tosses it to the far end of the backyard.

And the sun—the sun shines the way sun always shines. And ravishing ladies continue to smell just as splendid as before.

—translated by Katie Farris and Ilya Kaminsky

THICKER
THAN WATER

by DANTIEL W. MONIZ

OUR MOTHER CALLS AT nearly midnight, well past her usual sleeping time, so I know something has a hold on her. Some bug or a ghost, sleepless itself and unrelenting. Me, I always was a creature of night.

"Enough," she says as soon as I answer. "You and your brother will make peace. You will spread your father's ashes in Santa Fe. Like he wished."

I pick at a pimple nestled in the folds of my left armpit. It appeared sometime during the course of the day, among the in-growns, a painful pink-white bump. I don't want to burst it, just suss out its particular shape. When I withdraw my fingers, they are damp and smell lightly of onion. I wipe them on my shirt.

"What about work, Mamá?" I ask, when work—my mutable employment as a dog walker and babysitter—would never be the issue.

"Just a couple of days. You can make the time." I can see what she looks like over the phone lines, the scarf covering her graying curls, her face determined, smooth at the jaw and sheathed in darkness. How her words are a prayer but also a bondage. "Cecelia," she says, "it's been too long. Your father needs rest." But what she means is, *We all do.*

After we hang up, I sit a moment holding my phone in both my hands. The flicker from the TV blues the room, accompanied by a nostalgic heaviness. My brother is of night, like me. For the last year, I have avoided thinking of him, across town, separate in his wakefulness. But our mother has summoned us, and there is no escaping that call. I dial. He answers on the second ring and this tells me he's been waiting for me, as I've waited for him.

"Lucas." His name feels unfamiliar in my mouth, a little sour, but with a honey to it; I haven't said it in so long. "Mamá just called." He sighs and it sounds like storm.

"I know," he says, and my silence concedes my utter secondness—in this news as in the order of our birth. Of course she called him first. I wasn't the child who needed convincing.

"So? Are we doing this?"

"Two weeks from now. I can take four days, no more."

Our mother wants us to drive. To really see the land, she said—the red hills and the cacti standing tall as soldiers—but we both know she wants us to share a small space. To have no other option but to mend. I sense every reluctance in him. His petulance is clear as a song, seeming stronger even than in those days when we were little and hassled each other over every inch of ground to give. Some grudges are like that. Fermenting in the long eye of time. But I won't indulge him. Not yet. I want to prod at him a bit, he being a natural extension of myself.

I tell him, smug little sister, "We'll take your car."

*   *   *

When Lucas turns up in the driveway of our grandparents' old house, where I live alone, he honks like a bad date. He hates coming inside, to this place where our father lived as a boy after our grandparents moved him from his beloved Santa Fe to Tallahassee. Nothing similar in the two places, our father often said, but the vigor of the sun. Sometimes I, too, felt our father's presence in the halls—a figure standing distantly, unmoving, one hand inclined upward and toward me, as if in a toast.

I appraise my brother through the windshield in the early morning light, my travel bag cocked against my hip. In the time since I've last seen him, he's grown a beard and shorn the waves of his head into a close fade, and because he is vain, everything is kempt. Through the glass, his face is willful. Apprehensive as a cornered animal. He is lovely. There's something I long for in that guarded look, and I hope I seem similar to him. I set my hair in braids last night and this morning let them loose around my chin. I wore extra-strength deodorant and foundation for the purple blooming beneath my eyes. I want to appear beautiful to him and without guilt, like someone who's been wronged but who can fathom forgiveness.

Lucas speaks first, sticking his head out the window. "You getting in or what?" He pops the trunk and I throw my bag in next to his and slide into the passenger seat and it's like old times, except everything has changed. An orange light glows on the dashboard. CHECK ENGINE. And I say, pointing to it, "Do you think we'll make it?"

Our mother opens the door even before we knock. She's packed us lunches in brown paper bags—ham-and-Kraft-cheese sandwiches and two tangerines each. She seems relieved to see us there together in her living room, even awkwardly, unspeaking, our bodies angled away from each other. Our pictures are everywhere, clearly dusted and attended to; us as kids, us as a family before fracture—evidence that we'd started somewhere and sometimes it was good. Lucas turns his face from it.

"We can't stay, Ma. We've got a lot of road to cover," he says, because he senses, as I do, that she wants us to linger in this past. He kisses her cheek to dull the rejection.

"I understand," she says, and hands the lunches to my brother. Then she turns and places our father carefully into my arms, the ceramic urn taped closed and wrapped in one of her good scarves. White linen with a pattern of peach dahlias, the bundle no bigger than a newborn child. She crosses herself, mumbling blessings into the air, and unlike Lucas, I can't kiss this away. Cannot turn my face. This is Arlo, our father, and he is everywhere in me. He taught me how to cook, how to type, how, when walking, not to look down at my feet. He was always precise with me and did not treat me as a child. He told me the names of things; when there was death he called it death. He upheld family above all else, and when he tucked me in at night he would say into my ear "Por la sangre," and wouldn't leave until I'd repeated it back. Until I'd made him believe that I believed it. I had loved him and was frightened of him, as he thought all good daughters should be.

Leaving, our father at my feet, Lucas turns the wrong way down the road.

"Freeway's the other direction," I say.

He rolls his eyes. "We've got one more stop to make," he says; then, "Hold on to that," speaking of the urn. I don't verbally respond, but bracket the bundle better between my sandals. An image rises up: the lid coming undone and our father's remains pluming across the floor mat among the lost pens, crumbs, and parking stubs. How we would look, stopping at the nearest gas station, inserting a quarter into the coin-operated vacuum. Our father funneling away as the one who was not cleaning leaned against the car and crunched a handful of BBQ Fritos. Arlo, in the end, just one more big, bad dust bunny. I laugh out loud because it's so unfunny, and Lucas shoots me a look like I've lost it. Maybe I have.

The house we pull up to is more of a bungalow than anything, painted sage, with a screened-in front porch and tie-dyed mandala sheets for blinds. On the porch I see an old patchwork couch, a lazy ceiling fan. There are books stacked on a milk crate at one end and a philodendron in a clay pot trailing its leaves through the speckled light. Lucas gets out and I realize his intention is to go inside. I realize he *lives* here, in this different place I do not know.

"I thought we were pressed for time," I say.

He's already moving toward the house. He says, "You can wait here if you want." But I'm curious. I follow him up the short concrete stairs, through the porch—it smells like rosemary and weed—and into the house. The living room is small but surprisingly homey. It feels airy, full of light. Unburdened by ghosts. Lucas disappears down a hallway and an orange-sherbet cat hops down from the TV stand to investigate, curling her small-boned body around my ankles. We stand and stare, both at a loss for what to make of the other.

"That's Lucy," says a female voice behind me. I turn to see a silver-haired white girl leaning against the wall of the hallway where Lucas went, and now everything makes more sense—the plant, the books, the cat. This co-op vibe. I should have known. When the girl moves into a patch of sun, I can see the curve of her cheek is faintly furred, like a peach. In the light, her hair becomes lavender.

"Oh," I say, and not wanting to appear startled or rude, I ask if the cat is named for Lucille Ball, that iconic redhead. She says, "No, named for the devil for her wickedness. I'm Shelby."

I tell her my name, that it's so good to meet her, when really what's good is that my brother brought me here, let me come in. A promising sign on our horizon. I'm making a note to tell him I appreciate this—once we're on the road, some miles between us and the strangers we've become—when Lucas appears again. A purple duffel stamped with heart-eyes emojis dangles from his hand. I look from his face to the bag. From the bag to the girl. "Sorry," she tells me with a crooked-toothed smile. "I was supposed to be waiting outside."

They leave a key under a loose floorboard so their friend can feed the cat. Shelby moves toward the front passenger seat and I can tell it's not out of spite but habit. Automatic shotgun. Girlfriend privilege. I brush pass Lucas as he situates her bag in the trunk and turn my face so there's little chance my lips can be read.

"This isn't what Mamá meant," I say, stoking the displeasure in my voice, and he bends lower into the trunk.

"You wanted to take my car," Lucas says. "My car, my rules." And I can't argue with that. These laws are nonnegotiable. When we're all buckled up and the engine is running, Shelby swivels and presents our father's urn to me, like she's offering a treaty. The mood between us feels that sacred.

"My condolences," she says, and I take him. After a moment I put our father in the seat next to me and buckle him in, too, so that every time Lucas checks his mirror for the road, he'll have no choice but to see.

Shelby doesn't believe in evasion, which I find out when I tell her how lucky it was she could get the time off work for this trip and ask her what she does. We're on I-10, driving west through the panhandle. Out the window, unremarkable stretches of field.

"I'm a foot-fetish model," she says, and I gawp at her rosy little toes, her feet propped up on Lucas's dash, old smudges on the windshield from past contact like abstract art. Her nails are painted a vivid, acid green, which is not her usual color. Her clients like French tips and hot tamale red. She tells me she had a friend who had a cousin who got her started, but after she blew up, she got her own site. Shelby breaks down the specifics of her job—the brand of pantyhose her clients prefer, the level of packages she offers, how much people pay for nothing more than watching her stroke Lucy's fur against her high arches. She explains the smelly-feet trope.

"Like, you know, I've just gotten back from a looooong run, and gosh, my feet are sooo tired, so sweaty, and then I make a big production of taking off my runners and my socks and all that. I can't tell you how many socks I sell." She says she does some of the normal shit too—lace and leather, *Oh baby I'm so hot for you*, just with more feet.

"It's great," she says, nodding. "It pays the rent and I can set my own hours. Plus all the cute shoes and pedis I want. You know, people will buy stuff off your Amazon Wish List."

I try to catch my brother's eye in the rearview, to see what he thinks about all of this, but he's resolutely not looking in my direction. I can't tell anything from the side of his face, but his right hand hasn't moved from Shelby's thigh. "What do you do?" she asks, and I say, "Basically clean up shit for a living. Play with people's fur and human babies." And she says, "That's awesome," like she means it and I find myself liking her for my brother.

By hour two of the drive, she's turned around in her seat, talking exclusively to me, as Lucas hasn't felt the need to participate. I appreciate her attention, which keeps me from feeling like a child in the backseat. It turns out Shelby is also a purveyor of random knowledge—interesting facts she collects off Wikipedia and Reddit chat rooms. She knows about wine-making, the chemical makeup of methamphetamine, what the stars of the *Real World: Key West* are up to now, and the Stone Age architecture of Roman Catholic churches. Shelby says, "So, I'm sure you've heard about all life originating in Africa, but have you thought about what that means? That, like, the first gods were black too?"

I can tell she's wanted to ask me this probably since we met. She wants me to know that she's an ally. That for her my brother is not a fetish. I want to tell her that she doesn't have to try so hard—Lucas and I both grew up exoticized in a mostly white school system, so this is far from our first white-partner rodeo. I want to tell her all the ridiculous things we've heard over the years as proof of allyship, but she's been nice to me, so I humor her. I tell her, "Gods often reflect the people who create them." I ask her more about herself, tell her what I've been up to lately, as if we were old friends catching up. I'm speaking to her, but I imagine her as a medium between Lucas and me, what I hope he has missed coming through a messenger he's more willing to receive.

The three of us have steel bladders, so it's a while before we stop. When we cross into Mississippi, we pull into a desolate gas station off the highway just outside Lucedale. We all get out to grab snacks and stretch our legs. Shelby and I walk to the restroom while Lucas pays for gas at the counter. The cashier's eyes flick over us, cowboy mustache bristling. He doesn't speak, only takes my brother's money. Once in the stall, squatting over the discolored seat, my curiosity is finally stronger than my repulsion, and I ask Shelby through the wall: "Did you meet my brother off the foot site?"

"Oh no," Shelby says, laughing. I can hear her wiping, flushing. "I never meet clients in real life." They met at Floyd's, a college club on the Strip where one of my brother's friends was DJing, and started dating just before our father died. She tells me that sometimes Lucas appears in her videos, faceless, doing things to her or letting them happen to him. I don't ask her any more questions, and speak just so she'll stop. "Lucas was never the jealous type," I tell her, which is true except when it concerned the affections of our father. While we're washing our hands with the diluted, scentless soap, Shelby asks, "What about you? Seeing anyone special?"

"Define *special*," I say, trying to sound light. My foundation is holding up and my hair still looks great. Maybe she'll think I'm a cool, shoot-from-the-hip, love-them-and-leave-them kind of girl. I haven't had a serious relationship since before our father got sick. And even then, I didn't like to lay myself out that way. Love requires a bareness, a certain pliability, and I didn't thrill at the possibility of being transformed or wiped away. I look at myself in the mirror but instead see Arlo's tired face—the drawn, long pull of it after he and our mother fought. The two of us are in the living room alone, late afternoon, the light amber in my hair while I play dolls at his feet. I am six and happy, and he clutches my chin and tells me, "If I could, I'd marry you."

Shelby lowers her voice conspiratorially.

"Okay, so here's a tip. Attraction is all about chemicals. We're just like animals, you know?" She explains that humans secrete pheromones in urine and in sweat, and even if we're not aware of it, our bodies react. "So," she says, "what I do is get that clean sweat after a light workout, spritz a little essential oil, but leave my original musk. Here, smell." She beckons me closer and lifts her arm, and to my own amazement I lean into her smooth white pit. Under citrus I detect a smell that's a cross between chlorine and celery. Not welcome, but maybe not unpleasant either.

"And that's how I got your brother." She winks at me and flips her thin hair, which moves and shines as if liquid.

"I'll keep that in mind." I wish I could unknow everything she's said, but her sharing has given us an allegiance to each other. As we walk out, she threads her arm through mine and I let her.

Back in the car, my brother cranks the AC and gives Shelby a look.

"You took long enough. I thought that clerk was going to shoot me."

"Sorry, babe," Shelby says, and pops the top on a can of seltzer. She offers him a swig, which he takes, then she reaches into the lunch our mother packed and grabs a tangerine. Once it's peeled and quartered, she guides a slice between Lucas's lips and the bright juice bursts across his chin. Shelby wipes it away and absentmindedly licks her finger afterward, and I look out the window because such lazy intimacy is too much to bear. "You want one of these sandwiches?" she asks me like they're hers to give, but I don't respond. I'm too busy wondering what it's like to be so comfortable in your own body that you don't try to mask the scents of its functioning. That you make a profit from it.

I was always fearful of my own smells—of how they condemned or conspired against me. Our mother instilled in me early what evils might come sniffing, though she never illuminated the specifics. In her stories, they were hungry shadows who preyed on incautious girls. What I knew, I learned from our father. *National Geographic*, two lions roaring on-screen, the male biting the lioness' neck. Arlo pointing, his dry voice in my ear: "They're having sex." It looked painful. Scary. Bad. This was the evil our mother meant.

I see myself, fourteen, fifteen, in the bathroom, perched on the closed toilet. My underwear are a tangle around my ankles and in the cotton seat, a teaspoon of off-white glop. Sometimes it had a shimmer like pearl, and when I brought it to my nose, it smelled of egg or nothing at all. Was it, and the place it came from, normal? A boy at school had just begun reciprocating my clumsy flirtations, and I needed to know. I call for my mother to join me, and when she enters, I can't look her in the eye. Already I know that what is between my legs is a hunchbacked sinner, a thing to hide, but I stand and face her, offering my underwear in one hand and parting myself with the other.

"Does this look okay?"

Our mother curls her lip, but even in the moment I don't think she means it.

"It's fine," she says, and leaves immediately, not wanting to perform the double work of shaming me, since I've already shamed myself.

Lucas insists on driving the entire first leg and pushes our half-and-half schedule an extra hour. The day is a blur outside the window, meaningless, the sky eventually reddening until it bleeds itself into a dusty orange. Shelby finally talks herself out by the time we reach Texas and now snores in the front seat. I like it this way; I can better interpret my brother's silence, which shifts and deepens like music as the hours tick by. It feels less hostile and more unsure, like a space I can slip inside.

Around nine we find a Motel 6 just outside of Dallas and Lucas rents two next-door rooms. Shelby wakes and we carry our things inside, which for me includes our father. The rooms are typically dank and eerie, but we weren't expecting much. I place the urn next to the ancient box TV.

"I'm starving," Shelby says when we regroup outside. We all are. We split our mother's sandwiches and the rest of the tangerines hours ago. There's a burger joint across the street, so we order doubles and triples, extra-large fries, even shakes, like we're celebrating. We take everything back to the hood of Lucas's car and eat together under a wink of yellow moon. Lucas and I sit on a concrete parking block and he rolls a blunt from weed they hid in a coffee can and my heart unfurls. My brother is soft when he's high.

"White Grape?" I say, pointing to the rolling papers. Those had been our favorites.

"What else is there?"

He licks the blunt and lights it, and after getting it started, hands it to me. The first hit rolls through my body clean as wind, and I hold it as long as I'm able. When I exhale the sweet musk, the night opens above us, wild and listening. We smoke the joint small. Everything is better—the burgers, the shitty motel. Ourselves. I look at Shelby, sitting cross-legged on the hood like an ornament or a seer, the way her pale belly folds over the denim waistband of her shorts. There's no shame in her. She smiles at me, then inclines her head toward my brother.

I say, "Remember that time you told me sugar ants were sweet? And I ate some?"

Lucas snickers, his body loosening with the laugh.

"You were such a dumb little kid," he says, smiling. "Ma was so mad."

Our father had been madder, his expression grave at the sight of my swollen mouth. He'd kissed my forehead before pulling his leather belt from its loops in search of my brother. I don't remind Lucas of this.

He says, "Remember Abuela used to call us both pequeño chucho for years, and we thought it was just a pet name until the Mexican cousins told us it meant we were mutts? And you cried!"

"We both cried," I say. "But then we pretended to be dogs that Easter. Howling and lifting our legs on the furniture. Remember everyone thought it was so funny except Abuela? Mamá said we hurt her feelings."

Remember. Remember. Remember. The black moccasin in the community pool. The PE teacher's false eyebrows. Lena Crosby and her pink-glitter thong. This part is easy, time breaking open to slurp us gently into the simpler past. Where Lucas and I had bitten and scratched and punched and kicked and tricked and teased each other and still we went to sleep side by side. Shelby listens, her presence gentle as a chicken's egg.

Lucas is still laughing about the last thing we've remembered when I say, "Do you remember the year he put the presents on the roof? Because we forgot to remind him to leave the window open for Santa?" We had no chimney and our father warned us that if we forgot, Santa would skip our house. Lucas goes quiet and I press him. "Remember? We woke up crying because the tree was bare but then he climbs up on the roof and there they all were in a plastic sack? We believed in Santa that year." My brother says nothing.

"Remember he used to sing to Mamá in Spanish on the porch after dinner? And at bedtime he sang us to sleep?"

"You and I remember things differently," Lucas says, and I'm offended that he thinks that memory would work any other way.

"But you remember por la sangre," I say, dangling the words before him like tainted bait. That saying had been as present as air, as our own thinking of ourselves. A command as much as a toast. Lucas spikes his burger wrapper to the asphalt and an ugly part of me hopes he remembers how he failed, and that it haunts him.

"What's it mean?" Shelby's question darts between us, a startled neon fish.

"Basically, 'blood is thicker than water,'" I tell her, but I'm still looking at Lucas, whose face is tilted to the stars.

Shelby scratches a scab on her ankle and her voice hitches an octave. "There are speculations," she says, "that that's a misquote. That actually the phrase might be 'The blood of the covenant is thicker than the water of the womb,' which would have the opposite connotation than how it's commonly used." She says that in Arabic lore it gets even stranger. They say, "Blood is thicker than milk."

But neither of us is listening to her. My brother is leaning away and I'm now on my feet. I can feel my eyes glittering, a tight fury around my body, black as that pool snake. I had wanted to spin him one more memory, something good that could ease this hurt—but my tongue feels bitten. I say the wrong thing.

"Remember what he looked like in the hospital the last time you saw him?" Lucas stands, too, and the night shrinks down until it traps us. We aren't touching, but I can feel his body shaking and, like a bat, I use this to pinpoint my own location. I feel blurry and grateful—how much love it takes to hate this much.

"I remember," Lucas says in a low, dangerous voice, and we broadcast the memory between us: our father attached to all those tubes and Lucas leaving, refusing to speak. Lucas, a perfect match. I run after him down the too-bright hall and grab his arm; I swing him toward me and his hand is balled into a fist. I clutch him. "Please do this," I beg, "please." It's a scene, some bad TV movie, but no one blinks an eye. This is normal here. People surge around us as if they are river and we are desperate stones. "Please," I say. "Por la sangre." And Lucas looks at me, and behind his quiet rage is an even softer sadness. He tells me, "Blood is thicker than water, but you can't drink it."

"Come on, we're all tired," Shelby says, and now she's the one tugging my brother's arm. Our moment breaks and I know that tonight I won't get what I wanted. Shelby collects our trash into a grease-stained bag and they turn to go. Our father taught me to swim, to play dominoes, how to pop the meat from a crab claw. Our father is waiting in my room.

"What did he teach you?" I call out after my brother, and he actually stops. He looks at me.

Lucas says, "How not to be a man."

In my room, I conjure the memory that would have saved us: Lucas and me, small, before our parents cut his hair. We are snarls of black curls and big, dark eyes. We are doppelgängers, genderless, whole. We wrap a sheet around our shoulders and climb into the kitchen cabinet, where we pretend we are unborn, and that we have always been together.

In the morning, I take the first shift. Lucas slouches in the passenger seat with his hand over his eyes like he's hungover, and Shelby sits in the back with our father between her thighs. Finally, there is desert and the sky is a blue wonder against the barren mouth of the road. Our silence feels complete here. We stop for packaged pastries, weak coffee, some gas. We drive. We stop to pee or pretend to, for just one moment alone. We drive. We say nothing. We almost burst from saying so much nothing.

We're on the 40, just past Wildorado, when Shelby lurches forward between the seats, her finger an arrow at the glass. "Look out!" she cries. I jerk the wheel to the right and swerve hard around whatever is in the road. We bump onto the shoulder and something pops, the car lurching, brakes grinding, and slide on the sand before we stop, dust feathering around us.

"What the fuck!" Lucas says at the same time I do. I take the key from the ignition. We get out to check the damage.

Shelby says sadly, "It was a coyote."

Lucas squats at the front right tire, and even before I ask, I know that was the pop.

"Jesus Christ," he says, his hands on top of his head.

"Why didn't you check this before we left?" I ask him, thinking of the orange light on the dash.

He says, "This had nothing to do with the check-engine light. You *hit* something."

"Fine, whatever. Let's put on the spare and get out of here." Already the sun is baking us, wanting to strip us to our basest selves. There's sweat in my hairline and on my upper lip. Today I am not beautiful.

"I don't have a spare," he mutters.

"What? Who travels without a spare!" I yell, and now we're squaring up, face-to-face and as close as we've been in ages.

"I didn't want to be out here in the first place!"

"If it weren't for you, maybe we wouldn't have to be."

This spawns the kind of quiet that's ripe for lightening. Lucas leans in even closer and whispers, "Just because you like to forget—because you like to play Daddy dearest—"

I strike his face, and when I do it, I mean it. The sting of the blow warms my palm and spreads, jubilant, through my body. This connection, however violent, is what I've been waiting for. What I've missed.

Shelby pushes between us, as if to protect us from each other, but when she stands facing me, her arms outstretched, I understand exactly what she's standing between and where her lines are drawn.

"Y'all cool off," she commands, all her wispiness evaporated. My brother and I are winded, both shocked, and in our separate skin my contact translates differently. Lucas swats the air.

"Forget this shit. You wanna go to Santa Fe? I'll drop you at the bus station."

Shelby tells him to stop it. She checks her cell phone, then his. "No service," she says. She takes deep yogic breaths. If she suggests I do this, too, I know I'll lose it, but instead she says she and Lucas will walk back to Wildorado.

We're not too far past. She tells me to stay with the car. Lucas and I neither agree nor disagree, but I fling open the car door and stretch sullenly across the backseat. Shelby digs through the glovebox and tosses something into my lap. A switchblade. She says, "Just in case," and they go.

Hot and exhausted, I stare at the sagging roof, blinking back despair, and now I'm with our father, the lions rutting in the tawny grass. The lights are off in the bedroom, so the creatures blaze. I am six and the dark is a jaw around me. In the shadows, our father transforms. He's only Arlo, and his close, adult musk overwhelms me. "They're having sex," Arlo tells me, his hand a dry heat on my belly, and when he says it, something I don't have language for enfolds me like a womb. His hand is still and conscious, with its own heartbeat, and I'm a good daughter—loving him and afraid. I am as still as his hand, but the dark swallows me all the same.

I claw up and out of this memory, back into the car, where, at least, there's light and Arlo is only ashes. Only father.

I know Lucas is bluffing. That Shelby will talk him down. They'll come back with the tire and we'll go on. We'll honor our parents' wishes. But I imagine myself rising, exiting the car and opening the urn, the small puff of dust like a constricted cough. I fish through the fine silt of our father, snatch a hunk of bone, and lay it on my tongue, the muscle flinching at his grit. And while he's still between my teeth, I tip the urn and let him go to roam this lonesome road with the other restless things.

My shirt is damp under the arms now, two dark patches growing like eyes, and I can smell myself. Root vegetable. Earth. A murkiness. I try to sink down into the depth of my own scent, try to linger, to like it. But it's too intimate and I'm an animal of habit. I sit up, scrabbling for fast-food napkins in the center console so I can blot away the stink. Outside the window, Shelby and Lucas are only specks converging on the horizon, at that particular distance where it's hard to tell if someone is walking toward you or away.

INSTRUCTIONS
FOR AN
EXPEDITION

by REIF LARSEN

I. GATHER ALL THE MAPS.

ROAD MAPS, FIRE MAPS, topographical, hydrological, meteorological, astrological, epistemological maps. Study these maps in firelight. Rub castor oil on your fingertips. Carefully fold the maps; place them in your father's leather suitcase. Other things enter the suitcase: a pocket knife, a bottle of red wine, a ring of skeleton keys, a jar of squid ink, a toy trumpet.

Move the suitcase from room to room. Use it as a pillow. Use it as a plate. Eat your dinner off it as you watch the election results come in. Put on your boots. Wander through the footpaths near your home. Run. Pant. Discover a dead cardinal, lying in the pine needles. Hold the body close to your face. It died without anger. Rub castor oil on its wings. Throw the bird into the sky. Watch as it joins the other constellations.

2. READ THE FIELD GUIDES.

They are out of print; you must find them in bookshops that smell of damp, of warbled bindings, of elbows worn from elbowing. Eventually you will find what you seek: a 1954 second edition of *A Pocket Field Guide to Crustacea of the Province Lands*. What joy! Scuttle around the house like a crab! Scuttle until your head crashes into vinyl, into ironing boards, into the aquamarine colander hanging on a nail. Turn on the faucets. Don the colander. Let the house flood. Days go by. You begin to understand the moon and tides, as all crabs do. The mail piles up. The walls begin to buckle and sag. The grandfather clock begins to drown. Invite over five friends who have never met each other but who have each, in their own way, made something sublime. Grab the suitcase full of maps as it floats by. Open the wine. Split the oysters. Hold hands and listen to the sound of the rising waters.

3. BUILD A DIORAMA.

Your friends tell you: "Everything can be learned from a diorama." The only way to know the Faraway Place is to re-create it exactly. Every blade of grass, every grain of sand, every dead cardinal must be correct, in miniature. This will take fifty-five years.

You build your diorama out of an old cardboard box that once held your telescope. Make many trips to the hardware store. Fall in love with Ed, the son of the hardware store owner, also named Ed. Ed (the son) never meant to be here; he was meant to be out west, searching for two-billion-year-old granite. But his father became sick and now he's stuck in a loop. He tells you the names of rock formations—Vedauwoo, Devils Tower, Washakie Needles—as he sells you card glue and one hundred X-Acto blades.

"Thank you," you say and ache like a vise.

The diorama takes shape. You have figured out a way to create a small weather system inside the box. It rains. The sun sets. There is an eclipse. Awe like syrup. One day you look inside and people have come to the shore in their boat. You are still building but they have arrived. They make little fires. They are bearded, dirty, weary from their travels. You carve out a kettle pond for them to get clean in. They scratch in the sand and watch the crustaceans burrow away from the light. You are getting to know this Faraway Place. In the evenings, these people, tiny, covered in fur, point to the sky and name stars. Sometimes you rattle the box just to keep them fearful. They fall to the ground and weep in terror. Tell Ed about these little people as he sells you glass beads that you will melt down to make more stars to be named. Ask about the health of his father. He shakes his head. Everything must be thrown into the sky eventually.

4. STUDY THE ARTISTS.

The artists are the only ones to be trusted. Copy their work. Use grease pens. Use a ruler. Rabbit-skin glue, squid ink. Run your hands across their pages. Buy their lost paintings at the Old Auction House on Shore Road. Read their journals. Cut out the drawing of the man lying asleep on the beach and tattoo it across the sole of your foot. Show the art to the people living in the diorama. They have advanced now. They no longer live in tents. They live in shacks, hotels, sleek glass cubes. They cook salmon using gas stoves. They sprinkle powder on their mustaches. They trim their hair. The people in the diorama look at the drawings of moon phases, toads, egg pigmentation. Some of them wander to the very corners of the diorama, where the light bleeds in through the cardboard seams. They begin to draw. You watch them. They cry, stamp, yowl. Most of them die. Some of them find ways out of the box and now live in the walls of your house. You can hear them scratching at night. They are the last of the artists.

5. PACK.

Pack your socks and a bottle of sand fleas into your father's suitcase. Pack a bell and a pair of pliers and a matchbook. You will not need these things but this is how packing works. Before you leave, go on your first and only date with Ed. Find yourselves on the end of a pier. Take his hand. Kiss so briefly that there is nothing left but the memory of a memory. Let his hand drop. The spell does not extend this far out to sea. Realize that love is a layer of clothing that can be stuffed into the bottom of the suitcase, like a raincoat.

6. GO.

To get to the Faraway Place you must build a longboat, as the original people did. Fill the longboat with all the things you will not need. Bring your father's suitcase. Bring the fallen limb of a linden tree. Bring the grandfather clock. It cannot tell time resting on its side. Lash everything together with the last of your goose twine. On the morning you leave, discover that Ed has left an envelope on the gunwale. Your name in perfect serif capitals. Inside there is a letter that you will not read.

The journey will take seven days if the winds are right. The winds are right. Smell the air as you get close. Watch as a cardinal falls from the sky into the hull of your boat. Watch as your boat begins taking on water. Squint. Tremble. You have come this far. But: there, in the distance. There are the Province Lands. Slide out of the boat like an eel. Leave everything behind. Swim and swim, the seaweed tickling your shins. Realize you will not make it.

This is when you feel it. The first ache of solid ground. The waves coil you ashore. Gasping, sand against tongue.

The beach is covered in driftwood, dress shoes, a soggy feather boa. You find a wristwatch, still ticking. Down shore, a woman stands, clutching a kayak.

She is headed to where you came from. You want to warn her. The sea is filled with movement; clocksprung bodies churn against the current.

Make a fire. Scratch in the sand, searching for crustaceans. Later, spot your father's suitcase, spinning in the shallows. Evidence from another world. The lock is rusted shut. Take a stone. Bang the lock and bang the lock and bang the lock until it cartwheels open. Inside you will find your maps. They are waterlogged and blurry, stained by time and tide. Blood and ink. Unreadable.

Still: find a room of white. Hang the maps on the walls. Rub castor oil on your fingertips. Throw dirt into the sky. Balance on your haunches. Now wait. Wait until the world begins to shake and then dive toward the light.

Adapted from remarks given fireside in the Dunes of the Province Lands, coinciding with the opening of *Expedition*, an exhibition by psychogeologist Mark Adams, on September 29, 2017.

A MAN FALLS ASLEEP

by DANIIL KHARMS

One day a man falls asleep a believer but wakes up an atheist.

Happily, this fellow keeps medical scales in each room, and has a marvelous habit of weighing himself each morning and each night. And, so, when he weighs himself at nights he finds he is 175 lbs. And in the morning, having woken up an atheist, he weighs himself again and discovers he weighs only 173 lbs.

"Therefore," he gleefully announces, "my faith weighs nearly 2 lbs."

—translated by Katie Farris and Ilya Kaminsky

ALL ADDICTS

by MICHAEL DEAGLER

LIKE ALL MAILMEN, MY father hated James Farley, William Kendall, and Herodotus.

His reasons were self-evident. Farley was the namesake of the James A. Farley Post Office Building in Midtown Manhattan. Kendall was the architect who inscribed the words across its frieze. Herodotus supplied the slogan: "Neither snow nor rain nor heat nor gloom of night stays these couriers from the swift completion of their appointed rounds."

"I can tell you that Herodotus never had a walking route in August" was something my father would say, and on that point I could hardly disagree.

My father hated, in particular, the currency of the words among the general public. He hated how people would recite them at him as he struggled through Pennsylvania's sundry elements. How they thought that in so doing they were being clever, or that they were sharing a moment of mutual under-standing with their beleaguered letter carrier. They were fools. There could be no understanding. Only a mailman could know the trials of mailmen. Even I, a mailman's son, knew them only secondhand.

"It isn't some oath," my father said. "It has no official status. They're words carved on a fucking building. Nobody told Kendall to put them up there."

"You know what bothers me about it?" I asked. I wanted to stand with him on the same side of an issue. "It sounds like it's going to be a couplet, but then it doesn't rhyme at the end. That feels like a missed opportunity."

"Have you found a job yet?"

I was living in my father's house again, at age twenty-six. He was unhappy about it. At twenty-six, he had been with the post office for four years. He was married and was renting an apartment. He had never been an alcoholic. He recalled these facts with some frequency to accentuate the differences between us.

"I have a job. I'm freelancing. It's a gig economy." I'd told him this many times before.

He was disinclined to believe me.

Other men my father hated were Patrick Sherrill, Cliff Clavin, and Charles Bukowski. He hated Steve Jobs, Jeff Bezos, and whoever it was who invented email. He hated people who thought the post office was a waste of tax dollars and that the whole enterprise should go the way of the Pony Express. "What the hell do they think this thing is about?" he asked me over breakfast. "The government fights the wars, paves the roads, and delivers the mail. Democracy or no, the government has always done those three things. It's been that way since the fucking Caesars."

There was no mail delivery on Sundays, which was why my father was present at the breakfast table. I was always present. My younger brother, Owen, had recently graduated from college, and he, too, had become a presence, chewing his toast with the false confidence of someone who still has his whole life ahead of him.

"Yo, Dennis, we're going to the Inn tonight," said Owen. "Having a going-away party."

"For who?" I asked.

"For me. I'm moving to San Francisco tomorrow with my buddy Logan. We're gonna get tech jobs."

"Good for you. That's a long drive."

"To the Inn?"

"To San Francisco. That's three thousand miles from here."

"Can't stay in PA," said Owen. "I'll end up working for the post office."

"I wouldn't let you work for the post office," said my father. He had jam on his nose, and a countenance that suggested it would be a mistake to inform him that he had jam on his nose. Another thing my father hated was the popular misunderstanding that a job with the post office was a good job. He was happy to detail why it wasn't. Downsizing. Shrinking benefits. Longer hours. Tracking devices in the trucks. "It's a shit job. There's no future at the post office."

"Dennis, are you coming or not?" asked Owen.

"To San Francisco?"

"To the Inn. I need a ride."

Since learning of my sobriety, Owen had taken to treating me as his designated driver. He liked to make me ferry him between my old haunts and watch my face stiffen with remorse. It used to be that I could tell him to fuck off, but the sobriety had flooded my system with a lot of useless empathy and brotherly concern. I often found myself on the verge of tears over all the love choking up my heart.

"I don't know what I'm doing later," I said.

"You're not doing anything," said Owen. "You got no job, no girl, no friends."

"I have a job. I'm freelancing. It's a gig economy."

"Maybe you should become a mailman. It's better than making excuses for yourself."

"Neither of you is becoming a mailman." My father said this because he cared about us. We knew that. "I'd rather you both ended up in the street."

Like all paralegals, my mother wore her resignation on her shoulders, tucked in underneath her tweed blazer. I never knew if she found it coarse or comfortable, but it lent a grim professionalism to her movements.

She did the work of a lawyer but did not receive the pay of a lawyer, nor the prestige of a lawyer; she didn't live in the house of a lawyer, nor did she have the family a lawyer might have. She worked for a credit card division that, over the years, had merged with one bank, then another, accompanied by the inevitable layoffs that her bosses promised would never occur. She had the dead eyes of a partisan who has survived more purges than luck should have allowed. She had coffee mugs stamped with the logos of her former employers: long-subsumed financial institutions like First Union, CoreStates, and Philadelphia National Bank. She leaned against the sink, sipping steam as it rose up from Wachovia, uninterested in making conversation on a Monday morning.

If she'd been surprised to see me return after eight years out of the house, my mother never revealed as much. For me, the narrative was one of shock and tragedy: an extraordinary young literature student from the suburbs who'd gone down to Philadelphia and drank himself into ordinariness (and then sub-ordinariness) until he'd been forced, due to a deficiency of skills and wits and second chances, back into the Bucks County subdivision of his youth. But on the day, six months prior, that I'd walked in from the train station, duffel bag in hand, she'd simply looked at me as though I'd returned from the grocery store absent whatever item it was she'd sent me to pick up.

"I put your books in the basement."

That was it.

Silence swung between us now. I struggled to remember if it had always been there. Perhaps I had desired it in the past, aided it with the reticence of my teenage years. Now I told myself I enjoyed it. A sober man's life was monastic. There was holiness in our abstinence from chatter.

"This is good coffee," I said in response to nothing. "You get this at Genuardi's?"

"Genuardi's is gone. It's a Weis now."

Other burdens my mother bore without complaint were the grocery shopping, the cooking, and the laundry. She bore gray hair dyed brown to conceal her mortality from her bosses. She bore the expectations of her dead parents, Irish Catholics born before the invention of love. She bore her commitment to the improved fortunes of the next generation, slippery as they were with ingratitude, liquor, and folly. She ignored the weight of these burdens. She willed it away.

Owen stumbled into the kitchen, destabilized by the symptoms of his hangover. His face contorted in the morning light as though he were an especially stoic prisoner recently released from a pit. I'd gone out with him the evening before to the Inn and half a dozen other places, though I'd spent most of my night smoking and spitting on sidewalks. It was his going-away party, I'd reasoned. I was obligated to see him off. Then the prick hadn't even had the decency to go away.

"You miss your ride to San Francisco?"

"I'm not going to San Francisco. Logan's an idiot. Those tech companies bring in talent from all over the world. You can't just show up in Silicon Valley and get a job off the street. I don't even know how to code."

"Maybe you can get a job in a mailroom. Work your way up. It's better than making excuses for yourself."

"They don't have mailrooms. They're tech companies."

"I know that. I was throwing your words back at you."

"Working your way up is a myth," said my mother. It surprised me, because she wasn't normally one to dismiss an idea outright. "There's executives and there's the rest of us. If you don't enter through the executive door on the first day, then you're the rest of us. You've got a year, Owen, to get on the executive track somewhere. If you don't, you'll be obsolete. Next year there's going to be a new class of college graduates even younger than you. Youth is the most sought-after commodity in corporate America. It depreciates quick."

Owen rolled his eyes. He retained that undergraduate quality of being unable to consider notions he found distasteful. "What about Dennis? Dennis is twenty-six and he doesn't even have a job."

At twenty-six, my mother had been employed, full-time, for eight years. She'd transitioned from high school student to self-supporting adult in that way people used to do. She'd had me and had gone back to work soon after. I don't say this to explain the distance between us. I really don't believe in that sort of early-childhood determinism. I spent a lot of time with my grandmother in those initial years. She was a kind woman. Never a harsh word.

"It's too late for Dennis," said my mother.

"Thanks, Mom."

"It's not the end of the world." She said it as though she might mean it. "I'd rather you freelance than work as a stooge."

"What about me?" asked Owen. "If I can't get an executive-track job, would you rather I freelance than work as a stooge?"

"Try to get an executive-track job," said my mother.

Owen probably believed, deep in the raw atria of his heart, that our mother loved me more than she loved him. But I knew, deep in the pickled ventricles of my own, that love had nothing to do with anything.

Like all recent college graduates, my brother was unsuited to most professions. He considered them beneath him, or beyond him, or outside his field of interest. If the purpose of a college education was to broaden the opportunities available to him as a worker, it seemed to me that he'd ended up substantially fussier than he'd been four years prior. Tell a certain type of young man he can do anything with his life, and he will petrify before your eyes.

A week later we were back at the Inn for Owen's second going-away party. I refused to buy him drinks, out of principle and out of penuriousness. Because of this, I felt as though I were witnessing the festivities from the outside. That was often how I felt in relation to my brother's life: like an impartial observer. We had different interests. Owen had played rugby in college. At the bar, he wore a rugby shirt with a Jameson patch on the chest. He had informed me recently that sobriety was for young girls and Protestants, and for that my father rewarded him with a snort of laughter.

Other things for which my brother was unsuited were magnanimity, mercy, self-awareness, and fraternal affection. He was unsuited for our small suburban town, where he would always be the son of my father, the son of my mother, the brother of me. He was equally unsuited for the larger world, where he could not depend on even those meager associations. You had to know him to like him. If you knew him well, there wasn't much to like.

I was more or less secure in bars. Sitting in a bar made me crave booze less than sitting at home by myself did, where I'd start to feel like somebody else's twenty-six-year-old disembodied thirst that had never been adequately quenched. The only perilous moment was the initial step over the threshold, when I would first see the whiskey bottles lined up on the shelves like Chekhov's foreboding arsenal, the incandescent light shining through the golden spirits like the Holy Ghost at Pentecost. But I could quell the impulse after a second or two. For an addict, survival is inaction. I would look at my hands. Look at my shoes. Find a seat. Find a drinking straw to smack across the thigh of my jeans as I jittered my leg into a state of ease.

The new plan was for Owen and his friend Jason to move to New York and get finance jobs. "You gotta already live in the metro to land a job in Manhattan. Jason's cousin works as a consultant or something. He's got an apartment in Murray Hill. Said we can crash till we land on our feet."

"Sounds like a leg up," I said.

"It's the center of the world." Owen said this as though he were espousing an original thought. "Let's do a shot. I can't believe you won't do a shot with your own brother before he moves to New York."

"I'm concerned that you don't understand how sobriety works. I'm concerned for what that means for your future."

"I'm trying to bond with you, you prick. You used to be fun. We used to have a good time."

That was ridiculous, of course. We'd never been close. We'd each wished to be closer, though never at the same moment. Now childhood had ended—several times over, it had ended—and intimacy proved to be another of those comforts reserved for other, better people.

I smacked my palm down on the scruff of Owen's neck, meaning for it to sting more than soothe. His shoulders shot up reflexively. "You'll do great in New York," I said. "You talk a lot and you lack empathy."

"Thanks."

It was a moment, of sorts.

On the drive home I stopped at the Wawa so Owen and his friends could piss out their lagers and replace them with meatball subs. I stayed in the car. It was my mother's car. Few things entreat a man to consider his life decisions more than sitting in his mother's car, watching a group of drunks awaiting their hoagies through a plate glass window, lit up like diorama models beneath fluorescent lights. I could hear the faint melodies of gas station pop over the deeper silence of the countryside beyond.

I used to think I should love this town, since it had made me and I was of it. Then I wondered if it was even possible to love the place you came from. So I went on not loving it—hating it, even—until I reasoned: who was I to hate an entire town full of lives and dignities that weren't my own? Since then I've ceased to engage with it at all. I've kept the town from my mind and have had no opinions of it. The town has responded in kind.

Owen got back into the car. He handed me a sandwich wrapped in crisp butcher paper. "Thanks for driving, Dennis. I got you this."

For a moment, my insides were again wet with affection. My perspective capsized, and those scenarios I was inclined to find wanting were suddenly bursting with promise and pinkish light. I felt that way sometimes, in that first sober year, when things were sometimes bewildering and sometimes appalling and oftentimes indeterminate and occasionally so elating that I believed that a whole litany of implausible and much-lauded concepts might be real and accessible to someone like me.

Then Jason got into the car. "Owen, did you gank my fucking hoagie?"

Like all addicts, I wanted nothing so much as for people to cut me some slack. Within the claustrophobic bosom of my family, there was a dearth of slack to be cut. It was sometimes best to get out of the house. The library was a good place for that.

I'd never considered myself a victim of anything other than circumstance, which is something that tortures all of us in significant if disparate ways. I'd endeavored to never blame anyone else for the way I was. I didn't quit drinking when I totaled a car at twenty-one, or when I lost my first job, at twenty-two, or when the booze killed (or helped to kill) my best friend at twenty-three. Any of those would have been a suitable place to disembark, but I felt as though I hadn't yet seen all there was to see. I liked to tell people that the thing that finally did it was that the only girl I'd ever loved got married to a guy who was a lot like me minus the alcoholism. But that wasn't quite the reason, either. Anyway, all of that had happened in Philadelphia, which was twenty-five miles and a lifetime away from my local branch of the Bucks County Free Library.

It isn't always something dramatic, is my point. Sometimes you just decide you want to live for a while.

I found myself in the Antiquity stacks, scanning spines for the name of that much-maligned anecdotalist from Halicarnassus. Herodotus's *Histories* is considered the urtext of the genre. The first instance of a person sitting down and trying to make sense of all that came before him. I hadn't read it, but I had read a book in college by Ryszard Kapuściński about how Kapuściński had read *Histories*, and I therefore felt like a minor authority on the work. I found a hefty copy, the faded letters of the title faintly registering against the age-darkened cloth, and flipped briskly through its brittle pages. It occurred to me to search for the postal motto, but I didn't know the context in which it had originally appeared. There was no listing for "post office" in the index.

"Is that Dennis Monk?"

At the end of the row stood Maeve Slaughtneil, with the leather strap of a messenger bag slung over the blade of one skinny shoulder. Maeve Slaughtneil: my classmate from grades one through twelve, in whose presence I had not found myself since high school graduation. She was a fixture of my childhood, in name if not usually in person. Our mothers had been friends, back when mine was young enough for friends to seem like a necessity in life.

"Maeve," I managed. "It's been a while."

"It has." She smiled like she was delighted to discover me there among the ancients. Maeve Slaughtneil, in the flesh. She looked good. Like... really good. I'd never thought so before. Sometimes you see something familiar recast in a new light, and it makes you suspicious of every thought and sense you've had in your life up to that moment. It still happens to me. It happened even more back then. I don't think it's a phenomenon peculiar to addicts. I think we're all similarly damned by it.

"Are you back around?" I spun my finger in reference to the Ptolemaic universe that centered on our town.

"Looks that way." She bit her lip. "Temporarily."

"Of course. For me too."

Other things I wanted from people included—well, nothing, really. Just some slack. They could keep their kindness, their pity, their advice, their commiseration. I just wanted to be left alone. Maybe a few minutes with another consenting adult. The booze more or less drowned my sex drive, or at least leveled my ambitions enough that I had been content to handle it mostly myself. Then sobriety came, and my long-dormant libido sprouted overnight like a mushroom from a wet lawn.

I would never have presumed to know what a woman like Maeve Slaughtneil was thinking, but it was apparently very near to what I was thinking (we were alike, it turned out, in many significant ways), and in what could not have been much time at all we were walking through her garage and into her parents' house.

"Is that Dennis Monk?"

This time the question was from Mrs. Slaughtneil, which should have been enough to chase me back out into the street, but Maeve managed to hasten me through the kitchen and down the basement steps, and I allowed myself to be hastened. Between the resultant sensitivity of my long drought, Maeve's unforeseen, aggressive efficiency, and the novelty of my partner and our location and general milieu, the rapture was over quick enough for me to wonder if it had really been worth the ramifications. But I almost always wondered that, after. As we caught our breath, I looked around at a basement furnished with an unreconciled amalgamation of baubles from a teenage girl's bedroom and the vestigial objects of a middle-class family's three decades of residency. Maeve's siblings were older. Out. Gone. Married? Maybe. Like they were supposed to be. Like we were supposed to be.

I regarded Maeve unfairly, as though she had made me an accomplice in some ill-considered crime that would tar us both irrevocably as undesirables. But we were undesirables already, like all mediocre people in a crowded world. All we had done with our quick, naked communion was confirm the conventional wisdom that people don't change. That we are who we are. That progress is a myth created to distract us from life's entropy. Maeve must have read all this, or something near it, in my face.

"Leave if you want to leave."

We were so close together—so unclothed—in a hallucination of intimacy in which I might have told her anything I needed to tell. But I did not. We were, maybe, too alike for that.

"No judgment," I found myself saying. "I'm living at home too. It's less than ideal, for this sort of thing. But I could never, you know, bring somebody over there. It'd be too weird."

"That's judgment," said Maeve.

Mrs. Slaughtneil watched me as I passed back through the kitchen.

She looked pained in that way mothers often are. "Tell your mom I asked about her."

Like all Irish Catholic families, mine was suspicious of admitted alcoholics.

Part of it was cultural defensiveness. Part of it was shame. Part of it was fear of the implied accusation that such an individual leveled at everybody else. Mostly, though, an admission of alcoholism meant that a series of frank conversations was unavoidable, and an Irish Catholic family dreads nothing so much as a frank conversation. We preferred to communicate our frustrations through parables, like "The County and the Roads That Weren't Repaved," or "Mr. O'Leary and His Fucking Dog," or "How the United States Post Office Bowed to the Insatiable Greed of Amazon."

"They're starting Sunday deliveries for Amazon packages," my father said. "Sunday. White trucks, blue uniforms, on the Sabbath. Because God forbide Amazon's customers wait an extra day for their crap. The weekend is over, boys and girls. The American labor movement is dead."

"Plenty of people have to work on Sundays," I said.

"Yeah? Do you?" The question sounded a bit like a shout. My father told his parables in a loud voice, for emphasis.

"With freelancing, you kinda work whenever there's a job—" I started, but my mother shook her head. I opted to proceed as a silent audience.

"Keep the working man busy so he can't start trouble," continued my father. "Just like in the old days, in the sweatshops and slaughterhouses. Make sure people are too tired to do anything but go home and go to sleep. No reading. No voting. No organizing. No speaking your mind. That's the fucking end of this fucking country. The camel's back just snapped under a truckload of Kindles."

Other suspicions held by my family included those toward corporations, Evangelicals, vegans, atheists, entrepreneurs, astrophysicists, and anyone who was good with money. Anyone, in other words, staking a claim on enlightenment. We didn't believe in enlightenment. Humankind was a gang of sinners, and there was no point pretending we weren't.

"I like to come home and have a beer," said my father, in light of nothing other than my continued presence in the room. He and my mother were seated at the kitchen table. I was preparing a pot of coffee by the sink.

"That's fine," I said.

"It helps me unwind." He was drinking a pale domestic lager brewed by a company that was owned by Belgians. My mother was drinking red wine from a box.

"That's part of the appeal," I said.

"You didn't used to be such a scold," said my father.

"I'm the way I've always been. I can only be one way." I tried to be forthright when speaking with them. This attempt to fix myself was a process of humiliation, I reasoned, so why not let my parents witness it? I had lost my right to parables. Fiction was more than I could be trusted with.

"Don't you have friends?" asked my father. "When I was your age, I was dying to get away and meet up with my friends." He winked at my mother. Now they were each other's only friend.

"Friends are overrated," said my mother.

"Mrs. Slaughtneil says hi." I watched the coffee trickle like snowmelt into the pot. I didn't even like the coffee. It was bad coffee.

"What does that mean?" asked my mother, as though I had spoken in code. "Is that a joke?"

"I saw her the other day. I was hanging out with Maeve, and I saw Mrs. Slaughtneil, and she told me to tell you hello."

My mother chewed on the inside of her cheek as she watched me from beneath weighted eyelids. "Maeve Slaughtneil is disturbed. What do you mean you were hanging out with her?"

"I ran into her at the library. What do you mean she's disturbed?"

"She's mentally ill." My mother spoke in a tone that suggested I might also be mentally ill. "She disappeared for three years. She was just released from a halfway house. She's still in her parents' custody, for Christ's sake."

"She's what?" I had not been aware of any of that. A side effect of my habitual inebriation was that it had kept me beyond the reach of most social memorandums, and I frequently failed to stay on top of my various peers' biographical developments. Or, if I did hear something, I tended to forget I had heard it. They say poetry is news that stays news, but, for a drunk, all news stays news. "When did this happen?"

"She moved back home last summer. It's a tragedy. She'll be the Slaughtneils' dependent for the rest of their lives unless they find a way to drug her back to normal."

Well, fuck.

Mentally ill how, exactly? As an addict, I was a font of empathy for the mentally ill of every stripe, but there were some people whose problems meant I probably shouldn't be sleeping with them. There were the ethics of it to consider. And the motivations of the other party. Was Maeve trolling for men at the library? And what the fuck was Mrs. Slaughtneil doing, letting her bring them home?

"Jesus Christ," I said.

"They say mental illness emerges in your early twenties," said my father, looking at me as though he didn't believe it. "You know what else emerges in your early twenties? Being a bum."

"Or being a mailman," I said.

"Bingo," he said.

*   *   *

Like all Pennsylvania towns, mine had been founded with the best of intentions, had then fallen short of expectations, and now existed in a state of gradual regress. Such was the fate of most Pennsylvania things and most Pennsylvania people. We like to joke about the Amish, but they realized long ago that if you ask for more than the minimum, you'll end up disappointed.

I was at the Inn again for Owen's third going-away party. This time the scheme was for him and his friend Morgan to drive down to Corpus Christi and get jobs on an oil rig. I failed to see the angle.

"Dangerous work pays a premium," explained Owen. "With my degree they'll probably make me a foreman. Two weeks on, two weeks off. Work a couple years, pay down my loans, get a nest egg going, invest that shit. Capital gains, Dennis. Earned income is for peasants."

"What if you blow up?" I was reasonably sure, by this point, that Owen wasn't going anywhere, so the occupational hazards of rig work were mostly an intellectual exercise.

"Who gives a shit? We all go sometime."

"Just seems a shame to die in Texas."

Other failures of my hometown were the three empty storefronts in our strip mall, the blank billboard on the northbound highway, and the condemned farmhouse across from our subdivision. And me. And Owen. He had chickened out of his New York plans. Our region's native inferiority complex had flared up and kept him home. At least that's how we had chosen to look at it. If something could be categorized as our collective failing, then it couldn't very well be blamed on us as individuals.

After the bars, Owen and I sat in the car in the Wawa parking lot. I wanted to smoke a cigarette, but we were in my mother's car, and only she was allowed to smoke in it. I could have smoked outside, but it was raining. I could have walked under the Wawa awning to smoke, but there were already a couple of drunks smoking under there. Drunks for whom I had even less patience than I did for my brother.

"Too bad Dad's asleep," said Owen. "He loves the rain."

"You know how it should go?" I was unconcerned about him following my train of thought, since being a sober man among drunks is tantamount to thinking aloud. "It should go: *Neither snow nor rain nor heat nor gloom of night stays these couriers from the swift completion of their FLIGHT. Night* rhymes with *flight.* Why would it be *appointed rounds?* It's like a misdirect."

"Well, it wasn't written it in English. Maybe it rhymes in Latin."

"Or maybe...," I said, thinking that perhaps life, in practice, was mostly about appointed rounds and not so much about flying. But I left the thought unfinished. Who was I, anyway, to finish a thought like that?

Raindrops passed through the beams of light emanating from the front of my mother's sedan. They sped resolutely toward the earth, only to be dashed to smaller droplets against the rough asphalt of the parking lot. How anti-climactic, to be born in a cloud and plummet through the immensity of the sky just to land among cigarette butts and candy wrappers and wads of gum. How inevitable.

"Hey, Dennis? Why'd you stop drinking?"

"To live for a while."

"So you like your life, then?"

"Not particularly."

"So why live, then?"

"I guess I don't want to get off before I see all there is to see. Especially if there isn't anything afterward."

Owen seemed to turn the words over in his mind. "Hey, Dennis?" He said it as though he were starting the conversation anew. "How 'bout this? I'll stay alive. And you stay alive. And that way we'll both have somebody. You know?"

"Sure." I appreciated the sentiment, whether or not it meant anything.

Owen seemed encouraged by my assent. "Hey, Dennis? Remember when we were kids?"

I thought about when I was a child. Addiction had provided the unexpected service of clearing my life of debris. It had demanded so much of my time—getting booze, drinking booze, finding ways to get more booze—that the nonessentials had fallen away like flakes of dead skin. Hobbies first. Excursions. Minor social obligations. Shallower friendships. Then those things I had once valued but for which I could no longer find the time. Books. Ambitions. The search for a significant other. I stopped observing every laundry day. I let my hair get long. Then it was jobs that went. Not good jobs, since I'd never had a good one. They had been the sort of jobs it was okay to lose. I bailed on plans. I stopped returning phone calls. The people who weren't in my life every day mostly ceased to be there at all. I didn't keep food in the fridge. I skipped a couple of showers. I didn't need to get out of bed every morning, not if there was already a bottle on the nightstand. I didn't need to be a writer, after all. The world outside my apartment began to vanish, then the world outside my room. Near the end, it was the past that I let go. My memories. My former selves. I had to lose them. I wanted to. It was too difficult to square them with who I'd become.

"No. I don't."

Like all histories, my family's seemed composed of a series of recurring mistakes that, while theoretically avoidable, tended nevertheless to repeat themselves. My grandfather was a mailman, for instance. And my grandmother, that kindly woman of my youth, took gin in her coffee. And nobody was happy, as far as I've been able to discover. Not in the way we define happiness today. They were mostly born before the invention of happiness. They lived and died comfortably in disappointment.

Owen and I drank our coffee at the breakfast table. It was a Sunday again, though my father wasn't present. There were Amazon parcels to deliver. The day was overcast, but dry, so at least there was that.

My mother leaned against the counter with her Wells Fargo mug. She wore a sweatshirt, one printed with the name of the college that I, and then Owen, had attended. It wasn't a very good college, and all of us knew it, and her wearing of the sweatshirt struck me as a bit like hanging a child's unschooled drawing on a cubicle wall. She didn't do it because she was proud of it. For her, it was a gesture of solidarity. She bound herself to us because she was our mother. Others might see it as an act of love. But love, I promise you, has nothing to do with anything.

"Two weeks is a long time to be at work," Owen was saying. "Even if you get two off afterward."

"It is," I said.

"And the pay's not that good, considering. I mean, for as dangerous as the work is."

"It isn't."

The light, in the morning, in the kitchen, was a thing I did not hate. There was something about the slant of it, the way the room seemed to glow from the floor upward toward the ceiling. I sometimes thought—in moments when I could sit in that kitchen alone, in the morning, when everyone was away—how tolerable it was. How sublime, even, if that doesn't sound ridiculous. I thought how, if it belonged to a different house, I would have liked for it to be my own kitchen. My adult kitchen, the kitchen for the rest of my life. And, really, the other rooms of the house were not so bad, divorced from their associations. I could have lived there happily had the house been in a different town. And even the town itself would not have been so undesirable, for all its failures, if only it had different people living in it than the ones I knew. And even those people could stay, all except for my family. And even my family didn't really bother me in the abstract, and I could conceivably have remained with them, if only they were different versions of themselves. But how simple it would be, I thought, to make the world tolerable—to make the world sublime—with only the smallest of adjustments. A shifting of the light, a rearranging of the furniture. A vaguely different shade for every painted surface. If the houses could all be turned a few degrees in some direction, and if the car interiors smelled faintly otherwise, and if the coffee was improved by a hair. If each person had a slightly different job, or a slightly different ambition, or comported himself in a slightly different way. If the chemicals in our drinks and in our brains behaved, and if we altered our expectations for their behavior. I could live in a place like that. I really could. I know how fussy I must sound, but everything is so, so close to perfect. Like a letter delivered only one house away from its correct address. Like someone you could almost love.

"So what now?" I asked Owen. "Where are you gonna go now?"

He shrugged. "I think I'll just hang around here awhile. Figure things out."

"No," said my mother. It surprised me, but it shouldn't have, because I didn't know her all that well. She looked at my brother. Looked at me. Pleaded. "You have to go now. You both have to go right now."

MUSIC TO BE PLAYED IF
I FALL INTO A COMA

by DAWN DAVIES

INSTRUCTIONS

SHOULD I EVER FALL into a coma, please enact the following measures, though I'd like to open with a quick semantic note: I'm not keen on the phrase "falling into a coma." One doesn't literally *fall into* a coma, because the brain doesn't go anywhere unless one falls into, say, a well, and the brain goes along for the ride and ends up in a coma as a result. One can also fall off a cliff, perhaps, or a bridge, or a ladder, or out of a tumbling car, or over the side of a bathtub, and *end up* in a coma, but I am not sure how the brain itself "falls" into a coma, though I understand we also say one "falls in love" or "falls asleep" when describing other neurological states of being. Interestingly, you never hear of someone falling into a seizure, or falling into a migraine. Still,

I don't like the "falling" reference for any of this. Never have. Falling isn't fun and you aren't in control, though this opinion will be of no import once I am in a coma. Note: though I do not anticipate falling into a coma, I do worry that writing about falling into a coma will make me fall into a coma, a double-edged sword with which the obsessive are often fraught. Let's knock on wood here.

Just in case, I have compiled a list of acceptable music to be played throughout the entirety of my coma, preferably through high-quality headphones. Seriously, if I end up in a coma, somebody please spring for the Audeze. You can get them online from Crutchfield. They cost four grand, which is about what my car is worth, but a coma would be an appropriate time for an extravagant purchase. Take out a loan if you need to, and I'll reimburse you when I get back from the coma. If I expire, either keep the headphones for your trouble or let my estate handle the reimbursement. They can sell my car. I once listened to "Little Wing" by Jimi Hendrix through a pair of Audeze and I felt like I was listening from inside his guitar.

Please also remember to occasionally rub the cartilage of my ears, because you know how achy they can become underneath a pair of over-the-ears headphones. Leave me about twelve music-free hours per night for healing my scrambled brain, yet feel free, whenever possible, to cover up the sounds of beeping with music. All beeping—the IV beeps, the ECG monitor's beeps, the nurses' cell phone beeps, the microwave-down-the-hall beeps. I hate beeps like I hate spirochetes and clowns and sandworms. Also, if I am sharing a room with someone who needs respiratory therapy, please play lively music during any suctioning. The only thing I hate more than beeps and spirochetes and clowns and sandworms, those sneaky bastards, is the sound of sputum rattling in a throat.

CAVEAT

Please note that the following music should not be allowed anywhere near my coma: Bananarama, Jethro Tull, Nickelback, Tool, Bartók, James Blunt, Stan Getz and João Gilberto, Astrud Gilberto, Biz Markie, Primus, Ariana Grande, Jefferson Airplane *and* Jefferson Starship, Philip Glass, Fine Young Cannibals, any death-metal or hair-metal bands, the Doors, Rod Stewart, Lady Gaga, the Fray, Skrillex, Diplo, Skrillex feat: Diplo, Diplo feat: Skrillex, or any combination thereof, the Moody Blues, anyone from *American Idol*, and Faith Hill (no offense to Faith Hill; I like her voice but I don't like what her producers do to her songs). Also, please do not include any musical group that hired anyone associated with the past or present engineering or production of the Smiths. Oh, and the Smiths. I worry that if I was played the wrong music, I would lose my bearings and would not be able to find my way back into the real world. Music can be that powerful.

THE LIST

- Yes—*Close to the Edge*. The entire album. Play it at least once per week. You either love Yes or you hate them. I love them. I used to draw their album covers while I listened to their music, alone in my little Florida bedroom, lost in the twin universe they created just for me.

  - ▲ Of note: Yes was the first band I snuck out to see, and when I say I "snuck out," I mean I snuck out of my bedroom at one o'clock in the morning to watch them on old reruns of the weekend TV show *Night Flight*. I was mesmerized. I could see hip bones and penis bumps through their spandex pants, which was scandalous and more frightening than anything else at age thirteen, but Yes's musicianship was extraordinary enough to make me wonder if they practiced so much that they forgot to eat. All the shag haircuts and the shiny capes, and the way that when Steve Howe played "The Fish" on his guitar his lips puffed out and he looked like a fish. I would turn the volume down low, prop my eyes open with my fingers, and watch them play together like they were sawing up a frozen woolly mammoth and their entire village depended on them for survival. I loved Yes so much, and I never did find anyone in my life to share that love with me. I tried friends, family, fellow musicians in school, and finally, when, years later, my own children asked me to please, please, please, stop playing that "god-awful sound" in the car on the way to school, I gave up. Now I listen to them in private, through my low-end headphones, and it makes me happy, though I'll bet they'd sound even better through the Audeze.

- The Champs—"Tequila." So I can picture Pee-wee Herman dancing in his white platform shoes through the flower-strewn landscape of my coma bar. Saturday nights only. Once at around nine thirty, and once around the time when you think last call would be. If you happen to be visiting and you are carrying a flask, go ahead and uncork it. Get a little crapulent, especially if you feel uncomfortable watching me twitch and grimace, or watching the nurses measure the contents of my urine bag, or if you can't stomach my mouth hanging open when they turn me for bedsores.

- King Crimson—*Discipline*. The entire album. Twice per week, but this is a heavy album, so if you suspect I am having a bad go of it from the inside—*por exemplo*, I might be at a location in the coma where I am sucker-punching clowns while swimming through clotted, bloody, spirochete-filled muck—handpick the songs.

▲ Of interest: Bill Bruford, the original drummer for Yes, left Yes for King Crimson after *Close to the Edge*, to create *Discipline* and other fine KC records, which supports my theory that Bill Bruford is a genius; therefore, I go where he goes.

▲ An aside: I listened to *Discipline* during my formative years as an aspiring musician, when my neuroplasticity was at its peak, and as a result I have retained every sound wave of this album. I have listened to it instrument by instrument during multiple road trips throughout the years. I know where the time changes are. I have cataloged the nuance of every lyric Adrian Belew says or sings to the point where I can say the spoken words in pitch as he says them, and I also regularly practice singing all the lyrics, usually while alone in my car. I know this album so well, I don't need to listen to it. I can re-create it in my head all on my own, if needed, which I have done, during long MRIs or at times when I have been stuck in a line without a book. Robert Fripp's repetitious guitar patterns have hypnotized me as if I were a puff adder in a basket and he were a turban-wearing snake charmer playing some sort of panpipe or whateverall get-out they play when they hypnotize snakes.

▲ Note: I know snake charming is a myth, and I know the cruelty with which snakes in these hypnotism shows are treated... They often have their mouths sewed shut, but forget that. *It's a coma we are dealing with here.* Let it go.

▲ Quick aside: I once tweeted King Crimson singer Adrian Belew, who is so versatile a player that he makes King Crimson, which is a four-piece band, seem like a seven-piece band. I was in South Carolina at the time, and he tweeted that he had had a fine weekend at Wofford College, which happened to be a half hour from where I lived, and I thought I had missed him in concert, so I boldly tweeted him to express my disappointment. He tweeted back telling me he had been visiting his daughter, who attended Wofford at the time. Kind, but trusting, I must say. My privacy paranoia would incline me to never publicly reveal the location of my children, but Mr. Belew, bless his heart, plays by different rules, though you can bet I googled his daughter just to see if I could find her. *I did.*

• Michael Jackson—*Thriller. Thriller* is practically a perfect record, thanks to the recording genius of Bruce Swedien, whose work I have informally studied, and to Quincy Jones, who is a genius and a half.

▲ Quick note: please use "Wanna Be Startin' Somethin'" as a periodic tester song. If I don't wag a finger or squeeze my eyelids together to the beat of this song, check my brain stem.

• Rush—*Exit... Stage Left*. The entire album. Seven times per week.

▲ Note here: feel free to play "Red Barchetta" multiple times per day. This is a musically complex, yet hopeful, positive song, the timbre and intensity of which I predict would inspire me from within the coma to begin to claw my way up and out of what I imagine would be a deep, vitreous humor of sludge, past the stretchy Cling Wrap top layer, or the kind of thick, sweet skin that forms on top of a bowl of pudding after it cools, or a thin, dried coat of Elmer's glue some coma villain has Zambonied all over the top of my coma. Sometimes a person can't get past a thing like that and may end up giving in. Also, feel free to make friends with any medical, paramedical, or support staff you happen to run into during your visitation time with me. The people in the white hairnets who drop off and pick up the trays of food, the ones who look too socioeconomically disadvantaged to ever become medical staff—they are some of the nicest people you could meet. I had that job once and I liked it.

▲ The nursing assistants are also good folks. They are the ones to have time enough to bring an extra blanket or adjust a loved one to a more comfortable position in the bed, or smooth dangerous nightgown wrinkles under a buttock, the kind that can turn a red mark into a life-killing decubitus ulcer. I worked this job, too, once upon a time, and aside from the perseverative fear of catching something from one of my patients, it was one of the best jobs I've ever had, because I liked helping people feel better. You don't have to perform a spinal tap on someone to do that. You can help them in simple ways, like bringing them an extra pat of butter for their potato or sitting with them for a moment while they complain about their inattentive medical team or their children who are waiting like buzzards for them to die so they can rip into the estate. Ask the nursing assistants about their kids and their own education plans. They are almost always either working two jobs or going to school at the same time. They also are probably at least bilingual, and possibly trilingual. Mostly street-smart bitches you'd like to have a drink with, but they won't be able to, because as soon as they get off their shift, they will race off, either home to their families or off to school.

▲ Incidentally, "Red Barchetta" is another splendalicious road-trip song, and I have played it often while riding along a dark highway, trying to rearrange aspects of my life. It should be a major part of my coma soundtrack. "Red Barchetta" turns my dark sky the kind of blue you can see only on a clear fall day, when someone is burning leaves in the distance and you are cold enough to think about pulling the hat and mittens out of your pockets, yet not cold enough to go inside. When you play Rush, the nursing assistants probably won't be thrilled, but put it on speaker and give it a go anyway. It's a good icebreaker, and I won't mind. If you have trepidations, try "Tom Sawyer." It's the song Rush will be stuck singing for the rest of their lives because everybody likes it, though in the original video, singer Geddy Lee looks like he could use some therapeutic myofascial release. This is not a euphemism for anything. His shoulders are just so tight.

• The following four songs: Skee-Lo's "I Wish," Barenaked Ladies's "One Week," House of Pain's "Jump Around," and Jay-Z's "Empire State of Mind," because I can perfectly rap all of them, and I like to rap when no one is looking, and a coma is the definition of a private venue. I can rap naked on the back of a Connemara coma pony and no one will see, and besides, at many points within my coma I expect to be spiked out to where I can trip a referee, so I need a coma soundtrack that will fit my coma state of mind.

▲ Of note: there is something about the trailed-off end of the scratching in "I Wish" that sounds like my grandfather whistling a ballad from the '40s, leaning against a curved wall with his hands in his pockets, a slight smudge far down the echo of a long tunnel, poised, waiting to meet me, if I could only get to him. It's been so long since we've seen each other. After he died, I had a dream where I met him when he was young—a rough-handed baseball catcher in the prime of his life, muscular back, flat stomach, tan skin, piercing blue eyes. We were at a party in his living room in Scranton, Pennsylvania. He wore white jeans and no shirt, and he glowed like he was lit from the inside by the Holy Spirit. I wore a white lightning princess gown that changed colors when I made the skirt swirl. He held his hand out to me and we danced. We knew information about each other that we never exchanged when he was alive. In this dream, before he slipped away from my grasp, I could see his soul and it was beautiful.

▲ I think a coma might be the kind of place you can wait in while you choose to get on the ride or walk back out and go the opposite way. Like a depot or an airport. Never the destination; always a place of waiting. Maybe there is a part of a coma that acts as a processing station, like Ellis Island or, say, the Atlanta airport—the place you go for a brief stop after a two-hour delay in Newark, and a brutal, child-filled flight, right before you get back to your people, no matter which side of the veil they happen to be on.

▲ Speaking of dreams, I once dreamed of a woman with long, stringy hair who wore a white, nearly see-through camisole. She was in a crowd, and when she turned around, I noticed she had black-and-gray angel wings tattooed on each of her scapulae. The next day, I went to a crowded street festival and saw a woman with long hair wearing a white, nearly see-through camisole. She turned and had colored angel wings tattooed over her scapulae. She saw me staring at her and gave me a menacing look, and we crossed paths ten or twelve more times that day, each of us pretending to ignore the other.

- MC Hammer—"U Can't Touch This." At least once per day, directly before something uncomfortable, like suctioning, or minor surgery to insert a J-tube, or neuro checks from the prick neuro resident everyone hates, the one who makes even the nurses roll their eyes when he leaves the room, his white coat pockets bulging with the kind of paper detritus residents end up slogging around, because his attitude is piss-poor and martyr-like and he thinks appearing burdened will make him appear more attractive, as in his mind the busiest people are the most important, even though, dude, *all* medical residents are busy and if you want to stand out, you should try hitting the gym, or getting your teeth cleaned, or paying a few more bucks for a better haircut, or maybe *being nicer to people*.

  ▲ "U Can't Touch This" is the kind of loin-girding song to be played before going out onstage, or before doing something unpleasant, like getting a digital rectal examination or having a stent pulled out of your kidney. This song is as dope today as it ever was. While inside my coma, I plan on morphing into one of MC Hammer's video dancers, the thickest, most muscular girl, the hearty one on the right who throws her shoulder and hair about, but won't show her stomach, though she should, the one *you know can eat*, the one who burns her intake like coal in a hot furnace because she goes *all out*. However unpleasant it might be within the coma at times, I would hope to be someone who puts on ankle-height, old-school black boots and a Lycra onesie to battle my way back out, if it turns out I want to. There may be a measure of choice in a coma that we don't know about from this side of things.

• Pink Floyd—"Comfortably Numb." Please keep the general Pink Floyd to a minimum, and don't feel sorry for me after learning the following: "Comfortably Numb" has been the theme song for my life. I know why this is, but I don't have time to explain it here. There is something dark about most Pink Floyd songs that doesn't belong in anyone's coma, specifically a quantity of dirty, nonmusical noise: groaning metal, chinging cash registers, ticking clocks, grunting hogs, and verbal vocal tracks underlying things in a way that makes listeners think they are hearing voices in their heads, though I think the engineering of their music is masterful and expert and ahead of its time. I wouldn't want to hear any animal sounds inside my coma, certainly not hogs, which feel a little demonic to me. However, you could play "Comfortably Numb" up to twenty times in a row, preferably when it is quiet in my room, and hopefully when it is quiet in my coma, though you would have no way to know when it is quiet inside the coma simply by looking at me. What is quiet, really? Does quiet mean silence? When I am in a soundproof booth getting my hearing checked, I can hear both the never-ending ringing in my ears and my heart beating like a nagado, *boom, boom, boom.* I have never experienced true silence, even in places that are promised to be silent, even though I have half the hearing of the average person. Even my dreams are chaotic and busy: sound waves bouncing off brain waves. I don't know what true silence is. I'm not sure it exists, even in a coma.

▲ Be careful, though: you could be sitting in the room, blasting the Pink Floyd to drown out the sound of the nurse suctioning the lungs out of the guy in the next bed. You might see a peaceful look on my face, yet inside my coma I could be screaming, running for my life while a large spirochete chases me down Coma Boulevard, past the fire station, past the coffee shop, past the strip of small, independently owned storefront businesses, past the woman with the angel-wing tattoos who trips me, stands over me with her knuckles on her hips, elbows bent, her dank hair hanging down, and punches me in the throat before throwing me into the woods, where a clown is waiting for me in a homemade fort half dug into the earth. Still, hope for the best. Play "Comfortably Numb." The string arrangements are simple and beautiful, and David Gilmour's first guitar solo renders language unnecessary, and his second solo sustains enough potential energy to explode the planet.

▲ Let's make a deal: if I cannot handle Pink Floyd from the coma, I would try my hardest to give you a sign: a lift of the pinkie, a grimace from the non-paralyzed side of my face, or a quiet storm of a fart, though don't always take a fart as a sign. I am a farter by nature, something I expect would continue throughout a coma, especially considering what a coma might do to one's loss of sphincter control.

• Haydn—all sixty-seven string quartets. I'd probably have the time, because: coma. Give me a break midway through, though. All that sawing on the strings might get to me.

• Bach—*Cello Suites*, Pablo Casals only. When I was a kid, I would ride my bicycle to the local library. It was small and offered the reasonable challenge of reading all the books in a given section, or listening to all the records they had, and for Bach, Pablo Casals is what they had, so I checked out the record, put it in my book bag, balanced the book bag on the handlebars of my bicycle, and rode home. No one in my family related to classical music, so I listened alone in my room until it was time to take the record back. Then I checked it out again. Casals's recording of the *Cello Suites* may or may not be the best, but I grew used to listening to his nuances and it's what I like. Twice a week with the Casals, please, unless you sense I might need to listen to it more often or less often. Look at my face. See if you might be able to divine anything meaningful in the tightness or the slackness of my facial muscles. See if you can tell if I am still there.

- Trick Daddy—*Thugs Are Us*. I know the whole album and love it.

  ▲ Note: Trick Daddy is from the 305, where I was from, too, until they gave everyone up in Broward County a different area code from Miami-Dade County, which pissed us off. Now I'm from the 954, which is not nearly as gnarly. Play "I'm a Thug" on the days physical therapy comes to stretch out my contracting limbs, or any other time you think I'd need the mental boost, because in my coma, I could be a muscly thug, unlike in real life, where I look something like Olive Oyl.

- Kelly Joe Phelps—*Roll Away the Stone*. The entire album. It's about resurrection and hope on some level, which might be worth thinking about in a coma. You listen to it, too, if you like. It's the kind of record that makes you wonder how an artist does what he does, and it will probably fill you with envy, while also making you warmly think of Jesus, even if you are an atheist and hate the thought of Jesus.

▲ I don't hate the thought of Jesus, but I wonder if he will make an appearance in my coma, or anywhere else in my life. I used to look for him all the time, in little things, or simple acts of kindness, great moments of salvation, but now I don't know.

• Art Blakey and the Jazz Messengers—*The Big Beat*. The entire album. I can take it all, though it is a little much energetically. Maybe Sunday would be a good day for this, or anytime it is nice out. I never was a drummer, but I'd be one in my coma while I still had the chance. Sometimes what someone does in her mind can be as real as what she does in her body.

• Afro Celt Sound System. Because I love their sound and no one will be able to make fun of me for listening to them when I am in a coma, like they do in real life. Perhaps I don't hang around the right people. This band is like pairing bacon with peanut butter. You wouldn't think it would be good together, but it is delicious. Like with Yes, I can't find anyone to hang out with who likes this music, so I listen to it alone. In fact, aside from solo road trips, when I stay in anonymous Red Roof Inns and am served at roadside diners by the kind of waitresses who show up in Ray Carver stories, a coma might be the only truly private place one can be in. You can do things in there that no one would ever know about.

▲ You can play every Afro Celt album. I am partial to *Seed* and *Pod*, and the collaboration with Peter Gabriel called "When You're Falling," a fitting song in this case. Play it over and over. The repetition will be no problem for me. If you must leave for a while, put the *Seed* album on repeat and go about your business.

- Lester Flatt and Earl Scruggs—*I Saw the Light with Some Help from My Friends*. The entire album. Give me a day or two or three between repeats, to let the twang die down. I'm a die-hard lover of bluegrass, but not the exclusive kind of die-hard who listens only to bluegrass, like those folks who don't have access to musical recordings in any form (MP3, CD, vinyl, Victrola) and must play the music live from their own porches.

  ▲ Note: this is probably the place in the coma where Angel Wings would show up and start a fight. She looks a little old-school Appalachian anyway, with her bony clavicles, and scraped knuckles, and that front-porch stare, and if she got in my face, I'd fight her out back of the coma playground. I would fight her hard, like I learned to do in the back of the recess area of my middle school when I was the new kid and was forced to fight the tough girl who challenged me. The adrenaline got me so hot I swung wide, missed the girl, and punched a recess lady in the boob, which won me street cred with the kids. If I went out behind the coma playground with Angel Wings, I think a lot would depend on my beating her. I beat her, I ride a victory sandworm out of the coma playground like in *Dune*.

- Everclear—*So Much for the Afterglow*. I'm picky about sound, and I have learned to identify the styles of engineers when I listen carefully enough. When I was really young, I liked everything Jimmy Iovine produced without knowing that he produced it, or that music producers even existed. I thought musicians just rented the studio and did their thing. I didn't like Patti Smith, but I loved her sound. I didn't love Bruce Springsteen, but his sound was so clean that I appreciated it. I listened to Stevie Nicks after she left Fleetwood Mac, and her sound was nuts. Iovine did all that, and besides, he did Tom Petty and the Heartbreakers, whom I love like family. Stan Lynch's drums are so isolated and sharp, like the edges of a cumulus cloud in a blue sky. It's like listening to music through a perfectly balanced crystal, as if Jimmy Iovine had OCD of the ear. He makes it sound perfect, which I need. My coma would need to be just right, which means the music would need to be too. Which brings me to Everclear.

▲ Aside: along with Radiohead's *OK Computer*, and a single of Wyclef Jean's mix of Whitney Houston's "My Love Is Your Love," *So Much for the Afterglow* was my primary divorce soundtrack. I played this album daily for about two years. I cried when I sang along to "I Will Buy You a New Life" because its perfect hopelessness described how I felt. During this time when I handed off the kids for visitation with their father, I would drive away blasting "El Distorto de Melodica." Sometimes I wouldn't go home. I would leave town and ride the country roads, blowing past startled cows, my windows rolled down, screaming all the violent instrumental parts over and over until I lost my voice.

▲ A secret: I went to high school with the guy who produced *So Much for the Afterglow*. In fact, I had a painful crush on him. There was no hope from the beginning, as I was as lanky as Taylor Swift, only with a crooked face and no access to a hairstylist. The crush was both talent- and wit-based. He was a very good musician, and had a dry, quiet sense of humor that I appreciated from afar. Once, in band class, when he heard the freshmen discussing *A Separate Peace*, which they were only partway through, he got up from the back of the room, walked down the risers and over to the chalkboard, picked up a piece of chalk, and wrote "Finny dies." Then he threw down the chalk, dusted off his hands, and walked back to his seat without saying a word. This made me love him and want to punch him at the same time, because I was one of the freshmen.

▲ Also: once, he had a house party and I went to it. Got dressed up in my WilliWear and ironed my near-fro. Not with a flatiron. We didn't have those. I ironed it with the same iron I used to iron clothes. I put my head down on the ironing board, laid my hair out on the board, put a wet pillowcase over it, and pressed the hot iron into my hair until I could smell it burning. The guy never noticed I was at his party, but that was the night I learned to drive a stick shift, so that's something. Note: this also is not a euphemism for anything. A very kind and patient older brother of someone I went to school with taught me on his blue Volkswagen Beetle.

• Earth, Wind & Fire—"In the Stone." To be played when any old high school friends have come to visit, though I don't expect I have but two who would. Earth, Wind & Fire is who you want if you need to dance while also pondering the deeper meanings of life, and to me, the abiding love represented in "In the Stone" is the kind of thing I'll be thinking about in my coma, though whose abiding love we are talking about is the real question here. Is it my family's? Is it God's? When it is time to leave the coma, would I be torn between going toward one or the other? Would I have a choice, or would it be like a pulling or, worse, a falling?

- John Mayer—"Heartbreak Warfare." Please, just the one song of his. I'm not a general fan, but he has a good, grainy, breathy voice, and the synthesizer and rhythm guitar do something driving, moving the song forward the way I think one might need in a coma, because a coma might give someone the opportunity to move forward to someplace new. Even if I moved backward in my coma and chose to wake up, my life would likely never be the same, so I would still be going someplace new. People don't just wake up from comas like they do on soap operas. They have wasted limbs, memory and balance problems. Anger issues. Damage. They need months or years of rehab. Maybe I wouldn't want that.

- Thomas Newman—"Drive Away" from the movie soundtrack to *A Series of Unfortunate Events.* You might not know him. Most people don't pay attention to the music in a movie unless it is terrible. I do, though, and this guy is a good composer. You can tell he has a wild mind from the sound combinations he is able to produce, but seriously: this song.

  ▲ Note: I suspect that if you are good at composing movie soundtracks, you can get rich off it, yet still be the kind of person who can walk unmolested through the grocery store. Seems ideal to me. Thomas Newman has a great setup. I have no idea what he looks like, and I won't google him, out of respect for that.

  ▲ Quick aside: I watched *A Series of Unfortunate Events* with my children after reading them some of the books. The movie frightened one of them, and she sat curled in a ball on my lap toward the end of the film. I understood the feel of the bones in her body, her hair, the sound of the breath that came out of her mouth, so intimately that I believe I will never know anything so well again. Sometimes I look for my babies in my dreams, now that my children are older and things have changed. Their ghostly forms are elusive, and I must work hard to chase them down, around corners, behind trees, behind dark shadows I can't see past. This seems like the kind of wistful mind game a coma would use to populate itself: my children, multiplied by the hundreds into every memory I have of them playing hide-and-seek, sitting down at the breakfast table, diving into a wave, crawling away full-diapered, felled by strep throat, cheeks flushed with fever, sneaking into my bed with a blankie, holding backpacks on the first day of school, getting their braces off, riding away on a horse, leaving for college. You can't underestimate how much you will miss the touch of your own child once they are gone, and a coma might be a controlled-enough place to realize the finality of their removal from your life.

• Mozart—*The Magic Flute* and *Eine kleine Nachtmusik*. I'm not full of classical knowledge or criticism, so I'm assuming this is pretty basic Mozart, which is fine with me. Play it all, but like with the Haydn, give me a break between the sawing bits. I might get tired in there, what with the clowns and the children and the rapping and the sandworms and the spirochetes and deciding whether to stay or drive away.

▲ Seriously: if we are on day 202 and I start to get a little bony, or people mention the name Terri Schiavo in reference to me, don't feel bad. Take a break if it is stressful. Don't visit for a week or so. I probably wouldn't notice, and if I did, I certainly wouldn't mind. I know what it's like to need a break. If you want to stay connected, listen to my playlist while you are running errands, or share some of the songs with your kids or your friends. I'll just be hanging around, looking for the promise of my grandfather, or chasing echoes of my children, or turning my face up toward the milky light that shines from the other side of the pudding skin.

- Peter Gabriel—entire discography. Play it whenever you want. It should line the streets of my coma. When I go into a field of coma flowers, I want to see Peter Gabriel's face where the head of every flower should be, surrounded by thousands of golden-lipped petals that sing tiny, complicated harmonies.

  ▲ Once, when I was in high school, I listened to Peter Gabriel's "Biko" for the entirety of a fishing trip to the Keys. I sat in the back of my stepfather's VW Vanagon and used my headphones to block out, like any good teenager would, the "new family feel" my mom was trying too enthusiastically to cultivate. When I listened to "Biko," I didn't care about divorce, or about my mother's new relationship, or about the new stepfather I hadn't asked for, though he would later turn out to be a good guy. I cared about apartheid, and about memorizing the drum patterns in the song, and about making it home to Fort Lauderdale without showing any emotion.

- Chuck Mangione—"Bellavia." To be played on repeat at sunset for one hour. One Christmas, I found Mangione's *Children of Sanchez* cassette wrapped in Santa paper at the bottom of my Christmas stocking. I didn't love the album, but I loved "Bellavia." I listened to it every night before bed. I made a mixtape consisting of only soft songs suitable for sleep, and I recorded "Bellavia" at the end. Every night I would prop the boom box up on my chest and fall asleep to the music, waking to the loud *pock* of the depressed PLAY button releasing as the tape stopped. I would startle upright, then rewind the tape to the beginning and play it again, falling back asleep to the promenade of the music partnered with my wispy-armed dreams. I did this for hours each night for about two years, until I got a Sony Walkman with headphones. I still do that today, only I use digital music on a tiny player, with even tinier headphones. No wonder there is no silence in my dreams.

▲ Of special interest: "Bellavia" is the kind of song that makes you think of things in terms of befores and afters, even though it has a cheesy '70s synthesizer in it. "Bellavia" is what I want to hear after battling the coma clowns. If "El Distorto de Melodica" is before, "Bellavia" is after. The thing you hear once the fever has broken, or the insomnia has given up its hold, or the hurricane is over, and the sun is slanting through a cloud and you have hope that all will be okay, if for a short while. Because maybe a coma battle is not the battle you think it is. Maybe the demon clown you have always feared is not a demon but a brawl-scarred Old Testament–style angel you must battle to gain entry into *the next*, the only thing that stands between your place on Earth and your place in the cosmos. Maybe she has wing tattoos over her scapulae, and has been near you all along, and is not the threat you once thought her to be. Maybe she has been your invisible protector. Maybe not, but hey: "Bellavia" is what happens when you touch the ladder, and your hand turns to gold, and everyone you know is at the top, arms outstretched, saying, "Come on, come on, hurry." Especially that little piccolo at the end. It makes *my* heart ache with hope, but if you are having trouble with any of this, just listen to my soundtrack and imagine me driving away, maybe in an old blue Volkswagen Beetle, or maybe a red Barchetta, fields of coma flowers turning their faces toward me as I pass. It'll be all right, no matter which direction I turn.

A WORLD WAITING
TO BE LIVED IN

by SHUBNUM KHAN

ONE

ONCE, ON A SUNNY afternoon in March, we were sitting in a coffee shop. I was drinking coffee, even though I did not like the taste. He wanted to say something and I knew it could be good or bad, although mostly I expected it to be bad. After a while he said, "I have been thinking about her a lot." And we both were quiet. Then I said, "You should contact her." Afterward, we drank our coffees and spoke about other things, but none of it really mattered anymore.

That was the second last time I saw him.

TWO

Once, my mother phoned the man we buy chickens from and she said, "Hello, is this the chicken?" And years later, when all my sisters are married, when I have grown up and my grandfather is already buried, every now and then, we tell this story and we laugh and laugh.

And sometimes, when my mother is in the right mood, she laughs too.

THREE

Once, quite a long time ago, he was going away and he had a little get-together. At that time, we were not anything to each other anymore. When I had to leave, I told him I had his book and he came with me to my car to get it. I handed him the book and we stood outside saying goodbye. He, for something to do, began to flip through the book as we spoke, and the note I had placed between the pages flew down to the pavement and we both looked at it.

I had not expected that.

I had expected him to find it much, *much* later, or maybe never. Or perhaps it would be found by some slim girlfriend in a slip, who I imagined would be picking through the books on his shelf while he slept in the other room.

We looked at each other and I laughed too quickly. I grabbed the paper, mumbled something about a bookmark. He looked like he was about to say something, like he knew, but I had already squashed the paper in my hand and we were not anything to each other anymore.

I cannot remember now what I wrote except that at the time it seemed like a very important thing.

FOUR

When we entered my grandfather's room the day after it happened, my father caught sight of his father's watch and he turned suddenly and stepped out. He walked away, overwhelmed.

I went to the shelf and turned the face around so his grief might be a little less.

FIVE

At the beginning of the month my parents do the crossword together. When they get their magazine from the post office, my father photocopies the cross-word and attaches it to a clipboard.

My father calls out the numbers and my mother reads the clues.

Sometimes my father asks my mother to repeat a clue. Then he cocks his ear and says he still cannot hear and she tries again and he says, "You don't have to shout. Just say it clearly." Eventually she spells out what he cannot hear or she cannot pronounce and then they are fine.

Quite often they lose the eraser and then they argue about who has lost the eraser and how often things are lost in this house and why doesn't anyone watch where they put anything and they become very cross, until one of them finds the eraser under one of themselves and then they stop arguing and they laugh and laugh.

SIX

The very last time I saw him, we were talking on the stairs outside my office and it felt very normal and it did not feel like the last time.

Later that day I remembered I had a hat to give him for his birthday and I messaged him to say so and I thought there would be another time but there was not.

SEVEN

Once, my father shouted to my mother from the other room that he had folded the towels and put them on top of the tumble dryer.

And I, in the kitchen, wiping the breakfast table, passed on the message to her. "He said he folded the towels and put them on the tumble dryer."

My mother, washing the dishes in the scullery, told me, "What? *He* didn't fold the towels. *I* did!"

So I shouted the message back to him, "She says, 'I folded the towels.'"

My mother, outraged, dropped the dishes in the sink, turned to me with suds up to her elbows, and said, "*You* didn't fold the towels. I did!"

EIGHT

Once, we were driving somewhere and I cannot remember exactly why but I started to cry. He turned to look over at me in the passenger seat and he said, "Don't cry."

He pulled the car over and we sat like that for a long time on the side of the road.

NINE

Once, my grandfather fell down. I tried to pick him up by myself but he was heavier than I'd expected. I lifted him to his knees but then I got stuck. And we stood there like that: his hands around my waist, his knees on the floor, smiling in a helpless sort of way. Finally I pulled him up by his armpits onto his feet and it was very hard and I thought I would not be able to do it.

For an hour afterward he sat on the edge of his bed and looked down and, from time to time, rubbed the back of his head. When we gave him water, he recited a prayer and blew into it and he kept trying to put the glass down on a table that he could not reach until I took it from him.

TEN

Once, my father was trying to tell a story and I cannot remember exactly what the story was about but he kept insisting that he knew a certain fact before he would begin the story and my mother kept interrupting him with the certain fact. My father became angry quite suddenly and shouted that he had already said many times that he knew the fact. My mother, who had not been shouted at for a very long time, turned away and announced that he had spoiled the new year.

Later, over breakfast, they did not say much to each other and I told them I thought they were both wrong: that she should have let him speak and that he shouldn't have shouted so loudly. My father turned to my mother and nudged her. He said they were equally wrong and would she be his friend again?

And my mother, who was buttering toast, said she would think about it.

ELEVEN

Once, when we had unexpectedly become something to each other again, we took a drive. We were both very nervous because we had not seen each other in a long time and many things had happened in between. We spoke too much and too fast and once, in agitation, I think, we even held hands, although it was brief. I did not ask him where we were going and I don't think he knew himself but we both knew it was important that we keep moving. The coast was very green and our windows were open and everything turned salty as the ocean came in. We drove very hard and very far and it felt like we were running from something.

After some time we became less nervous and stopped talking as much and I think for a while we were silent and it was just the road ahead and the ocean inside the car. Slowly I started to relax and maybe he even switched the radio on and maybe we even made a joke. We spoke about our families and our friends and the people at his work and we did not speak about the things that had happened in between. He began to slow down and it no longer felt like we were fleeing something but like we were moving toward something.

The road started to narrow and the trees began to thicken and somehow we ended up by a large building. We jumped out and went into the gardens of this building as if we had always planned it this way. We walked among the flowers and pathways and watched tourists take photos. We did not say much but I think if you had laid a hand on our chests you would have felt both our hearts beating very hard. We stood on a bridge and on the green horizon before us we watched birds in the air.

And I cannot remember now how long we stood there except that in that moment we felt like small fluttering things in the wind.

On the way home, I'm not sure why but I asked him about what had happened in between and he did not answer, no matter how many times I asked, and so I knew. We were quite near my house by then and I became angry and started to shout. He turned to me and I saw that he was crying, which was very strange because I had never seen him cry before, and I'm not quite sure why, perhaps because he had no right to, I started to cry too. I told him to stop the car, that I wanted to get out, that I needed to get out immediately. But he kept driving until he was at my house and I jumped out and slammed the door without looking back and he drove away angrily. I went into the house and switched off my phone and I couldn't eat or sleep for the rest of the day.

The next day, or maybe the day after, we made up and then he had to leave again. And I don't think we were ever quite right after that.

TWELVE

Once, I was waiting outside the airport with a small crowd. It was dark and cold and there were many stars in the sky above. I had a sign in my hand, printed at the last minute. Beyond the small building, a plane landed and my heart began to beat so loud I thought everyone could hear. A troop of passengers came out the door and I tried to peer over the heads as I made my way to the front. I pushed through a crowd of men who were mainly taxi drivers and found a place to stand. I held the sign over my face and I stood there smiling and when one of the drivers looked over at me, I pointed to the sign and said, "It's a joke." He didn't understand but I was laughing and behind the sign I was a world waiting to be lived in.

SONNET

by DANIIL KHARMS

A wondrous thing occurs to me: I suddenly forget which comes first—7 or 8.

I run to my neighbors to see what they have to say about this.

And all they say, to my amazement, is that they, too, have no idea which comes first, 7 or 8. They can't recall a thing. All they say is 1, 2, 3, 4, 5, and 6. But the rest? Nothing at all.

We all run to a supermarket and shout to the cashier our predicament. The cashier smiles sadly. She takes a small hummer out of her mouth and, moving her nose slightly back and forth, whispers:

—In my opinion, a seven comes after an eight, only if an eight comes after a seven.

So happy. We are so happy. We thank her and we thank her again and we run out of the supermarket and then—and then—we all stop. We are sad because we look at each other and see that her words are devoid of any meaning.

What to do?

What, what, my sweet people, can we do?

We go to the summer garden.

We start counting the trees.

But reaching a six in count we stop and start shouting. What is next? A seven? A seven, some shout. Eight, spit others. Eight.

We shout.

We shout.

And then, by some sheer luck a child falls off a park bench and breaks both of his jaws.

What a lovely distraction.

We can all, finally, go home.

—translated by Katie Farris and Ilya Kaminsky

THE
APARTMENT

by T. C. BOYLE

WHO WAS TO KNOW? She might have outlived most of her contemporaries, but she was so slight and small, almost a dwarf, really, her eyesight compromised and her hearing fading, and if she lived a year or two more, it would have been by the grace of God alone. Yes, she was lively enough, even at ninety, wobbling down the street on her bicycle like some atrophied schoolgirl and twice a week donning her épée mask and fencing with her shadow in the salon of her second-floor apartment, overlooking rue Gambetta on the one side and rue Saint-Estève on the other, but his own mother had been lively, too, and she'd gone to bed on the night of her seventy-second birthday and never opened her eyes again. No, no: the odds were in his favor. Definitely. Definitely in his favor.

He turned forty-seven the year he first approached her, 1965, which meant that at that point he'd been married to Marie-Thérèse for some twenty years,

years that had been happy enough for the most part—and more than that, usual. He liked the usual. The usual kept you on an even keel and offered up few surprises. And this was the important thing here, the thing he always liked to stress when the subject came up: he was not a gambling man. Before he'd made any of the major decisions in his life—asking for his wife's hand all those years ago, applying for the course of study that would lead to his law degree, making an offer on the apartment they'd lived in since their marriage—he'd studied all the angles with a cold, computational eye. The fact was, he had few vices beyond a fondness for sweets and a tendency to indulge his daughters, Sophie and Élise, sixteen and fourteen, respectively, that year (or maybe they were seventeen and fifteen—he never could quite keep that straight; as he liked to say, "If you're very, very fortunate, your children will be twelve months older each year"). He didn't smoke or drink, habits he'd given up three years earlier after a strenuous talk with his doctor. And he wasn't covetous, or not particularly. Other men might drive sleek sports cars, lease yachts, and keep mistresses, but none of that interested him.

The only problem—the sole problem in his life at that point—was the apartment. It was just too small to contain his blossoming daughters and the eternally thumping music radiating from their bedroom day and night, simplistic music, moronic, even—the Beatles, the Animals, the Kinks, the very names indicative of their juvenility—and if he wanted a bigger apartment, grander, more spacious, *quieter*, who could blame him? An apartment that was a five-minute walk from his office, an apartment that was a cathedral of early-morning light? An apartment surrounded by shops, cafés, and first-class restaurants? It was, as they say, a no-brainer.

He put together a proposal and sent Madame C. a note wondering if he might see her, at her convenience, about a matter of mutual interest. Whether she would respond or not, he couldn't say, but it wasn't as if he were some interloper—he knew her as an acquaintance and neighbor, as did just about everyone else in Arles, and he must have stopped with her in the street half a dozen times in the past year to discuss the weather, the machinations of de Gaulle and Pompidou, and the absurdity of sending a rocket into space when life here, on terra firma, was so clearly in need of *immediate attention*. A week went by before he heard back from her. He'd come home from work that day to an empty apartment—Marie-Thérèse was out shopping and the girls were at rehearsal for a school play, but the radio in their room was all too present, and regurgitating rock and roll at full volume ("We gotta get out of this place," the singer insisted, in English, over and over) until he angrily snapped it off—and he was just settling down in his armchair with the newspaper when he noticed her letter on the sideboard.

"Cher monsieur," she wrote in the firm, decisive hand she'd learned as a schoolgirl in the previous century, "I must confess to being intrigued. Shall we meet here at my residence at 4 p.m. Thursday?"

In addition to the contract he'd drawn up in advance—he was an optimist, always an optimist—he brought with him a bouquet of spring flowers and a box of chocolate truffles, which he presented somberly to her when she met him at the door. "How kind of you," she murmured, taking the flowers in one all-but-translucent hand and the box of chocolates in the other and ushering him through the entrance hall and into the salon, and whether by calculation or not she left him standing there in that grand room with its high ceilings, Persian carpets, and dense mahogany furniture while she went into the kitchen to put the flowers in a vase.

There was a Bösendorfer piano in one corner, with a great spreading palm—or was it a cycad?—in a ceramic pot beside it, and that, as much as anything, swept him away. To think of sinking into the sofa after work and listening to

Bach or Mozart or Debussy instead of the Animals or whoever they were. And so what if no one in the family knew how to play or had ever evidenced even the slightest degree of musical talent—they could take lessons. He himself could take lessons, and why not? He wasn't dead yet. And before long the girls would be away at university and then married, with homes of their own, and it would be just Marie-Thérèse and him—and maybe a cat. He could see himself seated on the piano bench, the cat asleep in his lap and Debussy's *Images* flowing from his fingertips like a new kind of language.

"Well, don't these look pretty?" the old lady sang out, edging into the room to arrange the vase on the coffee table, which he now saw was set for two, with a blue-and-rose Sèvres teapot, matching cups and saucers, cloth napkins bound in silver rings, and a platter of macarons.

He sat in the armchair across from her as she poured out two cups of tea, watching for any signs of palsy or Parkinson's—but no, she was steady enough—and then they were both busy with their spoons, the sugar and the cream, until she broke the silence. "You have a proposition for me, is that it?" she asked. "And"—here a sly look came into the flickering remnants of her eyes—"I'll bet you five francs I know what it is. I'm clairvoyant, monsieur, didn't you know that?"

He couldn't think of anything to say to this, so he just smiled.

"You want to make me an offer on the apartment, *en viager*—isn't that right?"

If he was surprised, he tried not to show it. He'd been prepared to condescend to her, as with any elderly person—politely, of course, generously, looking out for her best interests as well as his own—but she'd caught him up short. "Well, yes," he said. "That's it exactly. A reverse annuity."

He set down his cup. The apartment was absolutely silent, as if no one else lived in the building, and what about a maid—didn't she have a maid? "The fact is, Marie-Thérèse and I—my wife, that is—have been thinking of moving for some time now." He let out a little laugh. "Especially with my daughters growing into young women and the apartment getting smaller by the day, if you know what I mean, and while there are plenty of places on the market, there's really hardly anything like this—and it's so close to my office..."

"And since my grandson passed on, you figure the old woman has no one to leave the place to, and even if she doesn't need the money, why wouldn't she take it anyway? It's better than getting nothing and leaving the place for the government to appropriate, isn't that right?"

"Yes," he said, "that was my thinking."

As far as he knew—and he'd put in his research on the subject—she had no heirs. She'd been a bride once, and a mother, too, and she'd lived within these four walls and paced these creaking floorboards for an astonishing sixty-nine years, ever since she'd returned from her honeymoon, in 1896, and moved in here with her husband, a man of means, who had owned the department store on the ground floor and had given her a life of ease. Anything she wanted was at her fingertips. She hosted musical parties, vacationed in the Alps, skied, bicycled, hunted and fished, lived through the German occupation and the resumption of the republic without noticing all that much difference in her daily affairs, but of course no one gets through life unscathed. Her only child, a daughter, had died of pneumonia in 1934, after which she and her husband had assumed guardianship of their grandson, until first her husband died unexpectedly (after eating a dish of fresh-picked cherries that had been dusted with copper sulfate and inadequately rinsed), and then her grandson, whom she'd seen through medical school and who had continued to live with her as her sole companion and emotional support. He was only thirty-six when he was killed in an auto accident on a deserted road, not two years ago. It was Marie-Thérèse who'd seen the notice in the paper; otherwise he might have missed it altogether. They sent a condolence card, though neither of them attended the funeral, which, given the deceased's condition, would have been a closed-casket affair in any case. Still, that was the beginning of it, the first glimmer of the idea, and whether he was being insensitive or not ("ghoulish," was the way Marie-Thérèse put it), he couldn't say. Or no, he could say: he was just being practical.

"What are you offering?" the old woman asked, focusing narrowly on him now as if to be certain he was still there.

"Fair market value, of course. I want the best for you—and for me and my family too. Here," he said, handing her a sheet of paper on which he'd drawn up figures for comparable apartments in the neighborhood. "I was thinking perhaps twenty-two hundred francs a month?"

She barely glanced at the paper. "Twenty-five," she said.

It took him a moment, doing a quick mental calculation, to realize that even if she lived ten more years he'd be getting the place for half of what it was worth, and that didn't factor in appreciation either. "Agreed," he said.

"And you won't interfere?"

"No."

"What if I decide to paint the walls pink?" She laughed, a sudden strangled laugh that tailed off into a fit of coughing. She was a smoker, that much he knew (and had taken into account on the debit side of the ledger). Yes, she could ride a bicycle at ninety, an amazing feat, but she'd also been blackening her lungs for seventy years or more. He watched her dab at her eyes with a tissue, then grin to show her teeth—yes, she still had them. Unless they were dentures.

"And the ceiling chartreuse?" she went on, extending the joke. "And, and—move the bathtub into the salon, right there where you're perched in my armchair looking so pleased with yourself?"

He shook his head. "You'll live here as you always have, no strings attached."

She sat back in her chair, a tight smile compressing her lips. "You're really throwing the dice, aren't you?"

He shrugged. "Twenty-five hundred a month," he repeated. "It's a fair offer."

"You're betting I'll die—and sooner rather than later."

"Not at all. I wish you nothing but health and prosperity. Besides, I'm not a betting man."

"You know what *I'm* doing?" she asked, hunching forward so he could see the balding patch on the crown of her head and the slim tracery of bones exposed at the collar of her dress, where, apparently, she'd been unable to reach back and fasten the zipper.

"No, what?" he said, grinning, patronizing her, though his stomach sank because he was sure she was going to say she was backing out of the deal, that she'd had a better offer, that she'd been toying with him all along.

"I'm throwing the dice too."

After he left that day, she felt as if she'd been lifted up into the clouds. She cleared away the tea things in a burst of energy, then marched around the apartment, going from room to room and back again, twice, three times, four, pumping her arms for the sake of her circulation and letting her eyes roam over the precious familiar things that meant more to her than anything else in the world, and not just the framed photos and paintings, but the ceramic snowman Frédéric had made in grammar school and the mounted butterflies her husband had collected when they first married. She'd been blessed, suddenly and unexpectedly blessed, and if she could have kicked up her heels, she would have—she wasn't going to a nursing home like so many other women she'd known, all of them lost now to death or the straitjacket of old age. No, she was staying right here. For the duration. In celebration, she unwrapped the box of chocolates, poured herself a glass of wine, and sat smoking by the window, looking out on the street and the parade of pedestrians that was the best show on earth, better than any television, better than *La Comédie humaine*—no, it *was La Comédie humaine*. And there were no pages to turn and no commercials either.

She watched a woman in a ridiculous hat go into the shop across the street and immediately come back out again as if she'd forgotten something, then press her face to the glass and wave till the shopgirl appeared in the window and reached for an equally ridiculous hat on the mannequin there, and here came a boy on a motor scooter with a girl clinging to him from behind and the sudden shadow of a black Renault sliced in front of them till the goat's bleat of the boy's horn rose up in protest and the car swerved at the last minute. Almost an accident, and wouldn't that have been terrible? Another boy dead, like her Frédéric, and a girl too. It was everywhere, death, wasn't it? You didn't have to go out and look for it—it was right there, always, lurking just below the surface. And that was part of the *comédie* too.

But enough morbidity—this was a celebration, wasn't it? Twenty-five hundred francs! Truly, this man had come to her like an angel from heaven—and what's more he'd never even hesitated when she countered his offer. Like everyone else, he assumed she was better off than she was, that money meant nothing to her and she could take or leave any offer no matter how extravagant, but in fact, if you excluded the value of the apartment, she had practically nothing, her savings having dissipated in paying for Frédéric's education and his clothes and his car and his medical degree—Frédéric, lost to her now and forever. She got by, barely, by paring her expenses and the reduced needs that come with having lived so long. It wasn't as if she needed theater tickets anymore. Or concert tickets either. She never went anywhere, except to church on Sundays, and that didn't cost anything more than what she put in the collection box, which was between her and God.

After Frédéric's death she'd reduced the maid's schedule to two days a week rather than the six she'd have preferred, but that was going to change now.

And if she wanted a prime cut of meat at the butcher's or *l'écrevisse* or even *le homard* at the fishmonger's, she would just go ahead and order it and never mind what it cost. Bless the man, she thought, bless him. Best of all, even beyond the money, was the wager itself. If she'd been lost after Frédéric had been taken from her, now she was found. Now—suddenly, wonderfully— purpose had come back into her life. Gazing out the window at the bustle of the street below, bringing the cigarette to her lips just often enough to keep it glowing, she was as happy as she'd been in weeks, months, even, and all at once she was thinking about the time she and her husband had gone to Monte Carlo, the one time in all their life together. She remembered sitting there at the roulette table in a black velvet evening gown, Fernand glowing beside her in his tuxedo, the croupier spinning the wheel, and the bright, shining silver ball dropping into the slot for her number—twenty-two black; she would never forget it—and in the next moment using his little rake to push all those gay, glittering chips in her direction.

He went to visit her at the end of the first month after the contract went into effect, feeling generous and expansive, wondering how she was getting on. He'd heard a rumor that she'd been ill, having caught the cold that was going around town that spring, which, of course, would have been all the more severe in someone of her age with her compromised immune system, not to mention smoker's cough. A steady rain had been falling all day, and it was a bit of a juggling act for him to balance his umbrella and the paper-wrapped parcels he was bringing her: a bottle of Armagnac, another box of chocolates (two pounds, assorted), and a carton of the Gauloises he'd seen her smoking on his last visit. This time a girl met him at the door—a woman, that is, of fifty or so, with sucked-in cheeks, badly dyed hair, and listless eyes. There was a moment of hesitation until he realized that this must be the maid he'd wondered about and then a further moment during which he reflected on the fact that he was, in a sense, paying her wages. "Is madame in?" he inquired.

She didn't ask his name or business, but simply nodded and held out her arms for the gifts, which he handed over as if they were a bribe, and then led him into the salon, which as far as he could see remained unchanged, no pink walls or chartreuse ceiling, and no bathtub, either. He stood there awhile, reveling in the details—the room was perfect, really, just as it was, though Marie-Thérèse, who'd yet to see the place from the inside, would want to do at least some redecorating, because she was a woman, and women were never satisfied till they'd put their own stamp on things—and then there was a noise behind him and he turned round to see the maid pushing the old woman down the hall in a wheelchair. *A wheelchair!* He couldn't suppress a rush of joy, though he composed his features in a suitably concerned expression and said, "Madame, how good to see you again," and he was about to go on, about to say, *You're looking well,* but that was hardly appropriate under the circumstances.

The old woman was grinning up at him. "It's just a cold," she said, "so don't get your hopes up." He saw that the presents he'd brought were arranged in her lap, still wrapped in tissue paper. "And I wouldn't have caught a cold at all, you know, if someone"—and here she glanced up at the maid—"hadn't carried it home to me. Isn't that right, Martine? Unless I picked it up by dipping my hand in the font last Sunday morning at church. You think that's it, Martine? Do you? You think that's likely?"

The maid had wheeled her up to the coffee table, where she set the gifts down, one by one, and began unwrapping them, beginning with the Armagnac. "Ah," she exclaimed when she'd torn off the paper, "perfect, just what a woman needs when she has a head cold. Fetch us two glasses, will you, Martine?"

He wanted to protest—he didn't drink anymore and didn't miss it either (or maybe he did, just a little)—but it was easier to let the old woman take the bottle by the neck and pour them each a dose, and when she raised her glass to him and cried, *"Bonne santé!"* and drained it in a single swallow, he had no choice but to follow suit. It burned going down, but it clarified things for him. She was in a wheelchair. She had a head cold, which, no doubt, was merely the first stage of an infection that would invariably spread to her lungs, mutate into pneumonia, and kill her sooner rather than later. It wasn't a mercenary thought, just realistic, that was all, and when she poured a second glass, he joined her again, and when she unwrapped the chocolates and set the box on the table before him, he found himself lifting one morsel after another to his lips, and if he'd ever tasted anything so exquisite in his life, he couldn't remember it, especially now that the Armagnac had reawakened his palate. He'd never liked Gauloises—they were too harsh—preferring filtered American cigarettes, but he found himself accepting one anyway, drawing deeply, and enjoying the faint crepitation of the nicotine working its way through his bloodstream. He exhaled in the rarefied air of the apartment that was soon to be his, and though he'd intended to stay only a few minutes, he was still there when the church bells tolled the hour.

What did they talk about? Her health, at least at first. Did he realize she'd never been sick more than a day or two in her entire life? He didn't, and he found the news unsettling, disappointing, even. "Oh," she said, "I've had little colds and sniffles like this before—and once, when my husband and I were in Spain, an episode of the trots, but nothing major. Do you know something?"

Flying high on the cognac, the sugar, the nicotine, he just grinned at her.

"Not only am I hardly ever ill, but I make a point of keeping all of my blood inside my body at all times—don't you think that's a good principle to live by?"

And here he found himself straddling a chasm, the flush and healthy on one side, the aged, crabbed, and doomed on the other, and he said, "We can't all be so lucky."

She was silent a moment, just staring into his eyes, a faint grin pressed to her lips. He could hear the maid off in the distance somewhere, a sound of running water, the faint clink of cutlery—the apartment really was magnificent, huge, cavernous, and you could hear a pin drop. It was a defining moment, and Madame C. held on to it. "Precisely," she said finally, took the cigarette from her lips, and let out a little laugh, a giggle, actually, girlish and pure.

Three days later, when the sun was shining in all its power again and everything was sparkling as if the world had been created anew, he was hurrying down the street on an errand, a furtive cigarette cupped in one palm—yes, yes, he knew, and he wouldn't lie to his doctor next time he saw him, or maybe he would, but there was really no harm in having a cigarette every once in a while, or a drink either—when a figure picked itself out of the crowd ahead and wheeled toward him on a bicycle, knees slowly pumping, back straight and arms braced, and it wasn't until she'd passed by, so close he could have touched her, that he realized who it was.

For the first eighty-odd years of her existence, time had seemed to accelerate, day by day, year by year, as if life were a bicycle race, a kind of Tour de France that was all downhill, even the curves, but in the years after she'd signed the contract, things slowed to a crawl. Each day was a replica of the last, and nothing ever happened beyond the odd squabble with Martine and the visits from Monsieur R. At first he'd come every week or two, his arms laden with gifts—liquor, sweets, cigarettes, foie gras, quiche, even a fondue once, replete with crusts of bread, marbled beef, and *crépitements de porc*—but eventually the visits grew fewer and further between. Which was a pity, really, because she'd come to relish the look of confusion and disappointment on his face when he found her in such good spirits, matching him chocolate for chocolate, drink for drink, and cigarette for cigarette. "Don't think for a minute you're fooling me, monsieur," she would say to him as they sat at the coffee table laden with delicacies, and Martine bustled back and forth from the salon to the kitchen and sometimes even took a seat with them and dug in herself. "You're a sly one, aren't you?"

He would shrug elaborately, laugh, and throw up his hands as if to say, *Yes, you see through me, but you can't blame a man for trying, can you?*

She would smile back at him. She'd found herself growing fond of him, in the way you'd grow fond of a cat that comes up periodically to rub itself against your leg—and then hands you twenty-five hundred francs. Each and every month. He wasn't much to look at, really: average in height, weight, and coloring—average, in fact, in every way, from the man-in-the-street look on his face to his side-part and negligible mustache. Nothing like Fernand, who'd been one of the handsomest men of his generation, even into his early seventies, when, in absolutely perfect health and the liveliest of moods, he'd insisted on a second portion of fresh-picked cherries at a *ferme-auberge* in Saint-Rémy.

She'd gotten sick herself, but she really didn't care for cherries all that much and had eaten a handful at most. Fernand, though, had been greedy for them, feeding them into his mouth one after another, spitting the pits into his cupped palm and arranging them neatly on the saucer in front of him as if they were jewels, pausing only to lift the coffee cup to his lips or read her the odd tidbit from the morning paper, joking all the while. *Joking*, and the poison in him even then. He spent the next six weeks in agony, his skin drawn and yellow, the whites of his eyes the color of orange peels and his voice dying in his throat, till everything went dark. It was so hard to understand—it wasn't an enemy's bullet that killed him, wasn't an avalanche on the ski slopes or the failure of an over-worked heart or even the slow advance of cancer, but cherries, little round fruits the size of marbles, nature's bounty. That had been wrong, deeply wrong, and she'd questioned God over it through all these years, but He had never responded.

When she turned one hundred, people began to take notice. The newspaper printed a story, listing her among the other centenarians in Provence, none of whom she knew, and why would she? She was photographed in her salon, grinning like a gargoyle. Someone from the mayor's office sent her a commendation, and people stopped her in the street to congratulate her as if she'd won the lottery, which, in a sense, she supposed she had. She really didn't want to make a fuss over it, but Martine, despite having fractured her wrist in a fall, insisted on throwing a party to commemorate "the milestone" she'd reached.

"I don't want a party," she said.

"Nonsense. Of course you do."

"Too much noise," she said. "Too many busybodies." Then a thought came to her and she paused. "Will he be there?"

"Who?"

"Monsieur R."

"Well, I can ask him—would you like that?"

"Yes," she said, gazing down on the street below, "I think I'd like that very much."

He came with his wife, a woman with bitter, shining eyes she'd met twice before but whose name she couldn't for the life of her remember, beyond "Madame," that is. He brought a gift, which she accepted without enthusiasm, his gifts having become increasingly less elaborate as time wore on, and his hopes of debilitating her ran up against the insuperable obstacle of her health. In this instance, he came forward like a petitioner to where she was seated on the piano stool preparatory to treating her guests to a meditative rendition of "Au clair de la lune," bent formally to kiss her cheek, and handed her a bottle of indifferent wine from a vineyard she'd never heard of. "Congratulations," he said, and though she'd heard him perfectly well, she said, "What?" so that he had to repeat himself, and then she said, "What?" again, just to hear him shout it out.

There were thirty or more people gathered in the salon, neighbors mostly, but also the priest from the local church, a pair of nuns she vaguely recognized, a photographer, a newspaperman, and the mayor (an infant with the bald head of a newborn who'd come to be photographed with her so that his administration, which hadn't even come into existence till three years ago, could take credit for her longevity). They all looked up at the commotion and then away again, as if embarrassed for Monsieur R., and there wasn't a person in the room who didn't know of the gamble he'd taken.

"Thank you," she said. "You can't imagine how much your good wishes mean to me—more even than the mayor's." And then, to the wife, who was looking positively tragic behind a layer of powder that didn't begin to hide the creases under her eyes, "And don't you fret, madame. Be patient. All this"— she waved a hand to take in the room, the windows, and the sunstruck vista beyond—"will be yours in just, oh, what shall we say, ten or fifteen years?"

If Marie-Thérèse had never been one to nag, she began to nag now. "Twenty-five hundred francs," she would interject whenever there was a pause in their conversation, no matter the subject or the hour of the day or night, *twenty-five hundred francs. Don't you think I could use that money?* Look at my winter coat—do you see this coat I'm forced to wear? And what of your daughters, what about them? Don't you imagine they could use something extra?"

Both their daughters were out of the house now, Sophie married and living in Paris with a daughter of her own and Élise in graduate school, studying art restoration in Florence, for which he footed the bill (tuition, books, clothing, living expenses, as well as a room in a pension on via dei Calzaiuoli, which he'd never laid eyes on and most likely never would). The apartment seemed spacious without them, and lonely—that, too, because he missed them both terribly—and without the irritation of their rock and roll it seemed more spacious still. If there'd been a time when he'd needed Madame C.'s apartment—needed, rather than hungered for—that time had passed. As Marie-Thérèse reminded him every day.

It would be madness to try to break the contract at this point—he'd already invested some three hundred thousand francs, and the old lady could drop dead at any minute—but he did go to her one afternoon not long after the birthday celebration to see if he might persuade her to lower the monthly payment to the twenty-two hundred he'd initially proposed or perhaps even two thousand. That would certainly be easier on him—he had his own retirement to think about at this point—and it would mollify his wife, as least for the time being.

Madame C. greeted him in the salon, as usual. It was a cold day in early March, rain at the windows and a chill pervading the apartment. She was seated in her favorite armchair, beside an electric heater, an afghan spread over her knees and a pair of cats he'd never seen before asleep in her lap. He brought her only cigarettes this time, though the maid had let slip that madame didn't smoke more than two or three a day and that the last several cartons he'd given her were gathering dust in the kitchen cupboard. No matter. He took the seat across from her and immediately lit up himself, expecting her to follow suit, but she only gazed at him calmly, waiting to hear what he had to say.

He began with the weather—wasn't it dreary and would spring never arrive?—and then, stalling till the right moment presented itself, he commented on the cats. They were new, weren't they?

"Don't you worry, monsieur," she said, "they do their business in the pan under the bathroom sink. They're very well behaved and they wouldn't dream

146

of pissing on the walls and stinking up your apartment. Isn't that right?" she cooed, bending her face to them, her ghostly hands gliding over their backs and bellies as if to bless them.

"Oh, I'm not worried at all, I assure you—I like cats, though Marie-Thérèse is allergic to them, but there is one little matter I wanted to take up with you, if you have a moment, that is."

She laughed then. "A moment? I have all the time in the world."

He began in a roundabout way, talking of his daughters, his wife, his own apartment, and his changed circumstances. "And really, the biggest factor is that I need to start putting something away for my retirement," he said, giving her a meaningful look.

"Retirement? But you can't even be sixty yet?"

He said something lame in response, which he couldn't remember when he tried to reconstruct the conversation afterward, something like *It's never too soon to begin*, which only made her laugh.

"You're telling me," she said, leaning forward in the chair. "Thanks to you, I'm all set." She paused, studying him closely. "But you're not here to try to renegotiate, are you?"

"It would mean so much to me," he said. "And my wife too." And then, absurdly, he added, "She needs a new winter coat."

She was silent a moment. "You brought me an inferior bottle of wine on my birthday," she said finally.

"I'm sorry about that. I thought you would like it."

"Going on the cheap is never appealing."

"Yes, but with my daughter in graduate school and some recent reverses we've experienced at the office, I'm just not able"—he grinned, as if to remind her they were on the same team—"to give you all you deserve. Which is why I ask you to reconsider the terms—"

She'd already held up the palm of one hand to forestall him. The cats shifted in her lap, the near one opening its jaws in a yawn that displayed the white needles of its teeth. "We all make bargains in this life," she said, setting the cats down on the carpet beside her. "Sometimes we win," she said, "and sometimes we lose."

When she turned 110, she was introduced to the term *supercentenarian*, the meaning of which the newspaper helpfully provided—that is, one who is a decade or more older than a mere centenarian, who, if you searched all of France (or Europe, America, the world), were a dime a dozen these days. Her eyes were too far gone to read anymore, but Martine, who'd recently turned seventy herself, put on her glasses and read the article aloud to her. She learned that the chances of reaching that threshold were one in seven million, which meant that for her to be alive still, 6,999,999 had died, which was a kind of holocaust in itself. And how did that make her feel? Exhausted. But indomitable too. And she still had possession of her apartment and still received her contractual payment of twenty-five hundred francs a month. One of the cats—Tybalt—had died of old age, and Martine wasn't what she once was, but for her part Madame C. still sat at the window and watched the life of the streets pulse around her as it always had and always would, and if she couldn't bicycle anymore, well, that was one of the concessions a supercentenarian just had to make to the grand order of things.

Monsieur R. didn't come around much anymore, and when he did, she didn't always recognize him. Her mind was supple still even if her body wasn't (rheumatism, decelerating heartbeat, a persistent ache in the soles of her feet), but he was so changed even Martine couldn't place him at first. He was stooped, he shuffled his feet, his hair was like cotton batting, and for some unfathomable reason he'd grown a beard like Père Noël. She had to ask him to come very close so she could make him out (what her eyes gave her now was no better than the image on an old black-and-white television screen caught between stations), and when he did, and when she reached out to feel his ears and his nose and look into his eyes, she would burst into laughter. "It's not between you and me anymore, monsieur," she would say. "I've got a new wager now."

And he would lift his eyebrows so she could see the exhaustion in his eyes, all part of the routine, the comedy, they were bound up in. "Oh?" he would say. "With whom?"

Martine hovered. The pack of the cigarettes he always brought with him lay on the table before him, and a smoldering butt—his, not hers—rested in the depths of the ashtray. "You can't guess?"

"No, I can't imagine."

"Methuselah, that's who," she would say, and break into a laugh that was just another variant on the cough that was with her now from morning till night. "I'm going for the record, didn't you know that?"

The record keepers—the earthly record keepers from the Guinness Brewery, that is, who were in their own way more authoritative than God, and more precise too—came to her shortly after her 113th birthday to inform her that Florence Knapp, of the State of Pennsylvania in the United States of America, had died at 114, making her the world's oldest living person. The apartment was full of people. The salon buzzed. There were lights brighter than the sun, cameras that moved and swiveled like enormous insects with electric red eyes, and here was a man as blandly handsome as a grade-A apple, thrusting a microphone at her. "How does it feel?" he asked, and when she didn't respond, asked again.

Finally, after a long pause during which the entire TV-viewing audience must have taken her for a dotard, she grinned and said, "Like going to the dentist."

Marie-Thérèse, who'd been slowed by a degenerative disk in her lower back that made walking painful, came clumping into the kitchen one bleak February morning in the last dwindling decade of the century—and where had the years gone?—to slap the newspaper down on the table before him. "You see this?" she demanded, and he pushed aside his slice of buttered toast (the only thing he was able to keep down lately) to fumble for his reading glasses, which he thought he had misplaced until he discovered them hanging from the lanyard around his neck. Marie-Thérèse's finger tapped at the photograph dominating the front page. It took him a moment to realize it was a close-up of Madame C., seated before a birthday cake the size of a truck tire, the candles atop it ablaze, as if this, finally, were her funeral pyre, but no such luck.

Whole years had gone by during which he'd daily envisioned her death—plotted it, even. He dreamed of poisoning her wine, pushing her down the stairs, sitting in her bird-shell lap and crushing her like an egg, all eighty-eight pounds of her, but, of course, because he was civilized, he never acted on his fantasies. In truth, he'd lost contact with her over the course of the years, accepting her for what she was—a fact of nature, like the sun that rose in the morning and the moon that rose at night—and he was doing his best to ignore all mention of her. She'd made him the butt of a joke, and a cruel joke at that. He'd attended her 110th birthday, and then the one four years later, after she'd become the world's oldest living human, but Marie-Thérèse had been furious (about that and practically everything else in their lives), and both his daughters had informed him he was making a public spectacle of himself, and so, finally, he'd declared himself *hors de combat*.

Besides which, he had problems of his own, problems that went far deeper than where he was going to lay his head at night—the doctor had found a spot on his lung and that spot had morphed into cancer. The treatments, radiation and chemotherapy both, had sheared every hair from his body and left him feeling weak and otherworldly. So when Marie-Thérèse thrust the paper at him and he saw the old lady grinning her imperturbable grin under the banner headline WORLD'S OLDEST LIVING PERSON TURNS 120, he felt nothing. Or practically nothing.

"I wish she would die," Marie-Thérèse hissed.

He wanted to concur, wanted to hiss right back at her, *So do I*, but all he could do was laugh—yes, the joke was on him, wasn't it?—until the laugh became a rasping, harsh cough that went on and on till his lips were bright with blood.

Two days later, he was dead.

At first she hadn't the faintest idea what Martine was talking about ("Dead? Who's dead?"), but eventually, after a painstaking disquisition that took her step by step through certain key events of the past thirty years, she was given to understand that her benefactor had been laid to rest—or, actually, incinerated at the crematorium, an end result she was determined to avoid for herself. She was going to be buried properly, like a good Catholic. And an angel—her guardian angel, who had seen her this far—was going to be there at her side to take her to heaven in a golden chariot. Let the flesh rot, dust to dust; her spirit was going to soar.

"So he's dead, is he?" she said in the general direction of Martine. She was all but blind now, but she could see everything in her mind's eye—Martine, as she'd been five years ago, hunched and crabbed, an old woman herself—and then she saw Monsieur R. as he had been all those years before, when he'd first come to her to place his bet. Suddenly she was laughing. "He made his bet; now he has to lie in it," she said, and Martine said, "Whatever are you talking about? And what's so funny—he's dead, didn't you hear me?"

Very faintly, as if from a distance, she heard herself say, "But his twenty-five hundred francs a month are still alive, aren't they?"

"I don't—I mean, I hadn't really thought about it."

"*En viager.* I'm still alive, aren't I? Well, aren't I?"

Martine didn't answer. The world had been reduced. But it was there still, solid, tangible, as real as the fur of the cat—whichever cat—that happened to be asleep in her lap, asleep, and purring.

NEW NIGERIAN VOICES

Featuring

OPE ADEDEJI

ROY UDEH-UBAKA

ADACHIOMA EZEANO

CHUKWUEBUKA IBEH

NGOZI JOHN

With an introduction by

CHIMAMANDA NGOZI ADICHIE

INTRODUCTION

by CHIMAMANDA NGOZI ADICHIE

EVERY YEAR, I ORGANIZE a writing workshop in Lagos. Thousands of people apply, many of them talented. But we have room for only twenty. In choosing the twenty, I look not only for good writing but also for courage and for what I like to call heart.

We spend ten days in a small hotel, around a large table, talking and laughing, reading stories from laptops and phone screens. We disagree and agree. We argue and explain. We talk about popular culture and politics. We break for lunch in the hotel restaurant, and pile our plates with rice and yams and plantains and vegetables. We take pictures. I ask about the poets they like and I ask about their love lives. We become, even if only briefly, a family.

This year, the tenth of the workshop, my friend Dave Eggers was kind enough to come and co-teach and to give these young writers a chance to have their first major publication.

I'm so delighted that these stories have found a home in *McSweeney's*.

I love the confidence, the clear-eyed honesty, the beauty, of these stories. In the early 1960s, with European colonialism ending all over Africa, Nigeria was at the center of a new African literary renaissance. But cultural production dipped with the military dictatorships of the 1990s, when little fiction was published. Today there is another renaissance, and it feels to me more resilient, more diverse, and with less of an obligation to overt politics. The young writers I have met at my workshops—like Ope, Roy, Adachioma, Chukwuebuka, and Ngozi—make it clear that our storytellers are here to stay.

AFTER THE BIRDS

by OPE ADEDEJI

THE SMELL OF AIR and taste of water make my skin crawl this morning. I know what's happened: I swallowed my key last night. I feel something move in my belly and I try several times to throw it up. While kneading my belly, bent over a bowl in the sink, a bird attempts to break in through my kitchen window. I look up as it dances around the mosquito net. It gives up, perches on the sill, and winks. I catch a glimpse of the trimmings of its blue contour feathers and the rings of orange in its eyes before it bobs its head and flies away. The quiet morning sun grows around it until it disappears.

I saw a bird just like this one following my Uber last night when I left Isaac's house. It was odd to see a bird's color blend with midnight's blue. It made a white mess on the windshield and danced around the side mirror until the driver did a sharp right swerve onto the expressway. At the time, there was no queasiness, and I know why: we do not always know in the moment that it's one in which everything changes—we did not use a condom last night and I am not on the pill. The bird continued to fly over us in the evening darkness until a police officer stopped the car to ask if we had anything or any person in the boot. My mind left Isaac's body and the sticky sweetness he pressed into me to focus on the possibilities of opening the Uber driver's trunk to find a body, curled, tied in chains, dead. A few years ago, during the bar exams, my roommate, a pregnant mother, was studying outside when she saw a bird drop dead and get caught in the clothesline. She ran into the house panting. The child in her womb heaved as she prayed for God to rebuke the evil sent from her husband's family to make her fail the exam or lose the new baby.

I wonder what the birds I see are saying to me.

During lunch at work, I break pieces of onion crackers into a white mug of creamy coffee because I can't eat anything else. This is how I know something is happening to my body, that my body is stringing things together like when a bird creates its nest—it creates a hole that can be filled only by certain kinds of food. The knowledge is impossible, too early, but I know. Gloria is by my side, in front of the coffee maker in the kitchen. She is going on about the metaphysical and juju. I wonder if she can tell I'm thinking of her brother, Isaac. Her face twitches when she talks about humans who identify as fairies, she says these things are real to them.

"Same way human birds or cat witches are real things to religious people," she says. Gloria's twitching distracts me from contributing. I wonder if she feels the twitching; I run the tip of my index finger over the coarse skin around her eyes to make it stop. It feels like I'm touching a bird's skin.

I cover my mouth and run to the toilet to throw up.

*   *   *

It's my Nikkah this weekend. I'm getting married to Hakeem, to his quiet eyes and to the tiny lump of flesh by his index finger that I like to lick. It's not that I don't love him. I do. But I love Isaac more.

I saw Isaac yesterday. I'll see him today and he'll come inside me like he did yesterday—our last gifts to each other, yes and amen. He's too wild to stay away from, but too cool on the tongue to be with forever. I met him at the nail shop on Admiralty Road, years ago. He'd come to get his nails done with Gloria; I looked up to see a square face with honey-brown eyes and textbook-asymmetrical features. They had an unsettling sameness to be just siblings.

I'd known Gloria for a few years before I met him. I'd first seen her face in a sultry Twitter display picture under the "Who to follow" list: lips black and slightly parted, face ashen, red 'fro, and eyes in a squint. Next, we swapped orange boots at National Youth Service Corps camp and took chilly 4 a.m. baths out in the open. We eventually became best friends over African and European fiction classics discussed in quiet conference rooms before staff meetings.

After we'd gotten new fingers, black for Gloria and Isaac, stiletto bright yellow with one finger bedazzled with gems for me, I invited them to hang out. I was housesitting for Hakeem, who was only an off-and-on boyfriend back then, so I said in a poetic voice, "Come and blend shadows with me under a bonfire in the yard." They stared at each other but he was the one who got lost in broken laughter. When they arrived at Hakeem's quiet house, we ate flowers and danced to frog croaks even though we were not high. The tall moringa tree with the empty nest watched us, and reported to Hakeem. It is the only explanation for the way Hakeem called, knowing I had guests.

"I'm glad you're having fun," he said. Oh, the sweet man.

The tree dropped tiny yellow leaves on us, mad. Isaac thought it wasn't safe and left the house. Gloria stayed close and kissed my back as I slept on wet grass.

We don't go to a bar, because Isaac doesn't drink anymore. It was his New Year's health-and-fitness resolution and he has stuck to it. He drinks only water and oranges, squeezed out without the pulp. We decide to ride one of the rickety boats behind his office, just so the water listens to our quiet.

Yesterday, we'd met up at Cactus, eating expensive fries and ice cream.

"I'm afraid of the jetty; it's steep and there are rocks under my feet," I say to him.

"You're being dramatic," he says. "It's your imagination."

He helps me put on my life jacket before we enter the boat.

"I met a bird," he tells me when we've both sat and the engine has started.

His face is softer than usual. His tongue is subdued; he doesn't look me in the eyes when he speaks. I conclude that he's sad I'm leaving him, getting married after several years of seeing him on the side.

"Hmm?" I respond, distracted.

"Yup. She told me some, um, interesting stuff about you, and, um, me."

I widen my cheek into a suggestive smile.

"I'm not lying," he says and turns to the water. His black skin burns under a stubborn sun but he doesn't sweat.

"Tell me?"

"Said we will never get married."

"That's why you're my side bitch."

He rolls his eyes. I wonder if that hurt him.

"Do you feel some way doing this with me while you're about to be married to him?" he asks.

"I've known Hakeem all my life," I say, then pause, contemplating the water. "Well?"

"I don't know how he'll feel if he finds out you and I slept together a few days before our wedding." I sigh before I continue, "I feel bad, a little. But we'll stay away from each other after the wedding, right? Besides, Hakeem and I are saving ourselves for marriage." I chuckle. "He should understand that I have needs."

Isaac doesn't reply. We are silent the rest of the time in the boat.

Two hours later, we are in the new building he runs his tech company from. His office is minimalist. My nude painting sits awkwardly on the wall behind a wooden desk. He painted it last month while I sat still, curled on the beach. My breasts seem bigger, my eyes too round, my tribal marks too small. The office smells of wood and of Isaac, who smells of Cantu. I'm going through the lease agreement of his building. He sits opposite me, fiddles with a bobblehead Obama, and nods to Niniola's "Dola." It's a terrible playlist. Simon and Garfunkel's "Bridge over Troubled Water" plays next.

"You know what I think?" he asks, turning down the volume of the music.

I take off my glasses, rub my eyes, clasp my fingers, stare at him—a concentration technique.

"I think we should do it again tonight."

I laugh. "Of course. Why do you think I'm here?"

"A last time before I die."

"What? What do you mean? Don't be like that just because I'm getting married, please."

"Um, it's not that. She said I'll die. Soon." His voice is raised now, but only slightly. He rubs his thumbs together. He looks exasperated.

"She?"

"The bird." He looks down at his fingers, my eyes follow his eyes; his nails are painted pink.

"I tried to follow her, ran down the road, then saw her hide behind an almond tree." He turns to the ceiling.

"And? Talk now."

"When I turned to the back of the tree, there was a woman dressed in a white garment, um, like cherubim and seraphim church clothing. She was holding a tambourine, singing. I couldn't possibly accost her, accuse her of being a bird."

"And?"

"And nothing. The bird was gone. Can we just fuck again? Forget about this bird and everything I've said. Yesterday was great. Didn't it feel good?"

I smile, then frown. "Tell me again where you first saw the bird?"

He points to the window.

The twins fought every day before they came out with round heads and sleepy eyes: Hassan and Hussain, Taiwo and Kehinde, Esau and Jacob. There was no question that they were the sons of their father, they had his complete hard-boiled egg head, but I saw Isaac in their eyes and asymmetrical features and wondered if it was a doubt I'd always live with.

The birds start to visit almost immediately. Hakeem starts a small garden, with pots of lilies, ixora, and aloe vera, and a wall of hibiscus, during the short paternity leave the bank gives him. His mother visits. She takes the twins and sits under the makeshift shade by the garden at midday, shaking her left leg. She tells me she is waiting. I don't know what she's waiting for, perhaps for the plants or the kids to grow. She's the one who notices the birds, how they flock around the shade and peer at the boys.

"It's nothing." I shrug. "Birds like flowers."

She's a superstitious woman who carries a bottle of holy water and sprinkles it around the house. She blesses the food the twins eat, calling up several gods to be their protectors even though it's mostly my breast milk.

She shakes her small head. "It's not nothing, my dear." It is something.

On a Tuesday a few days before Christmas, when the babies are six months and still boring—except that they can smile to show dimples like Isaac's—Hakeem's mother takes them out. She puts gloves on their hands and ties a cashmere scarf around her neck even though the heat slices the midday air. She doesn't tell me where they're headed. She smiles white lines and I itch to tell her to use a lip balm.

"You need a break, Arin," she says.

She tells me they'll be gone for three hours. "Rest," she says.

It's my first time alone since they were born. I've had a hunger inside since before they came that's made me restless and broody. It's not that the sex with Hakeem is bad, Isaac and I just have more sexual history; he knows my body better.

When the sound of Hakeem's old car has left the yard, I shave my vagina and apply red lipstick. I'm still in my housedress, the blue playsuit I bought bend-down-select from Yaba market that I wear in the kitchen when I'm not tying a wrapper. I don't think it matters. I'm not even wearing a bra. Before I start the car, I notice a hawk's beak protruding from the roof of the building. I bend to get a closer look. Its talons are curled on a rod at the edge of the orange roof. It looks down on me, or my car, not smiling or frowning, just looking, perhaps even curious. After I start the ignition, I look up to find that it's gone.

When I get to Isaac's office, it is locked. A heavy padlock is on the black gate. There's an inscription written in chalk on it: "This House Is Not for

Sale, Beware of 419." Below the words are torn campaign posters of the new APC candidate for governorship. And below them is a pile of junk—Lucozade, canned beer, pure water nylons. It's very unlike Isaac to allow his building to crumble to this state. There's no one anywhere on the quiet street to ask. I wanted my visit to be a surprise, so I hadn't called before coming. I try to call now and his phone is switched off.

Except for a brief peck at the naming ceremony a few months ago, I haven't seen or spoken to him since the day at his office. He did not show up for my Nikkah and did not send apologies. Gloria often keeps me up to speed, but since she moved away to Canada, it's been quiet. Social media helped too. I used to stalk his activities on Instagram, my eyes lingering on his imperfectly shaped face for a while, until I got bored with social media, its deliberate pretentiousness, and decided to invest more time in reading fiction.

I head home a little worried and twice as stressed. Driving in Lagos is a nightmare. The heat makes me dream of food. I stop by a grocery store to buy foodstuff for dinner. I want to make yam porridge, the kind that is peppery and has chunks of fish and vegetables. When I get home, the gate man tells me there's someone waiting to see me by the garden. I wonder who.

I burst into laughter when I see him. His face is bright, sawed to smoothness, a deep contrast to the white agbada he wears. He tells me he's coming from a wedding, and has to make a quick stop at a funeral after he leaves me. I don't ask who died. My mouth is too watery for questions. Isaac, my friend and possibly the father of my children, is here. I hug him tight.

He tells me I smell of crayfish and that my hair is a mess.

"The bloody thing," I say running my fingers through tufts of hair. "I'm going to cut it soon sha."

"Motherhood has really bent you."

I poke him. I don't want to think about it, how I have stopped working even though Hakeem didn't say I should, and how I no longer care about my looks. We sit on a bench in the garden, staring at the flowerpots next to us.

He takes my fingers in his hands and draws circles around the lines on my flattened palm. We are quiet, listening to the berserk birds above us and the intermittent sound of bangers exploding around us. Christmas songs from the flat above float down to us but we don't hear them. He still has that subdued look on his face, but now he wears it with wise eyes, a full Afro, and a beard. He brings his face close to mine, brushes his lips against my cheek. I close my eyes, thinking of the time his skin touched mine in his office, how his tongue danced down my body and made my toes curl into complete circles.

We stay like that for a while, listening to each other's breathing.

"I'm sorry I was not there," he says into my ears.

He stops short of saying *for you*, because he knows it could be the plural "you," *you and my kids*. I shrug. He's here now, isn't he?

"I really missed you," I say.

"I missed you too. I didn't mean to stay away."

I don't want him to talk about his pain. I clasp his fingers.

"Did you change your number? I tried to call you. I have just been to your office."

I don't think it is strange that we made to see each other on the same day after months of quiet. I believe in things like this—love of my life, soul mates, love at first sight, love that transcends.

"I changed it," he says. There's a maturity in his mannerisms that had not been there when I saw him before my wedding or even when he came for the naming ceremony in jeans and a hoodie. There are so many words to say and yet so few come.

"I'm afraid to die," he says.

"Stop it," I say, drawing away from him.

"You won't even ask why?"

I roll my eyes. "Why?"

"It's just that ever since that bird told me I would die, I've just felt like I would."

"What a foolish bird. Those things are manipulative. It's been what? Fifteen months? Yet you're not dead. You're healthy, aren't you?" I am wearing the thick tongue I've been preparing for when my children are older and I need to scold them.

He sighs.

I ask if he wants something to drink. He asks for water, smiling. He follows me into the house, sidestepping lizards and inhaling the thick harmattan smell. He plucks a hibiscus and sticks it into my hair. In the kitchen, while I pour him a glass of water, he stands behind me. He drinks up the water in no time. We stand in that position, his hand on my hip, my hair in his face, his crotch against my ass, breathing each other's fragrances. He smells of plants and of sunshine—natural yet so unnatural. He cups my breast and kisses my neck. I moan. I'm so in tune with his body that I don't hear the crying, the bang of the screen door, and the footsteps that make their way into the kitchen. He does, and dismantles his body from mine.

Mama walks in, flustered. Her cashmere scarf is now askew on her head and her white buba has several wet stains. She almost doesn't notice him.

"Your children are so stressful, ah," she says, pouring herself some water from the dispenser.

"Your grandchildren, Ma." I hide my voice inside my chuckling.

She looks up at him through round horn-rimmed glasses. "And who do we have here?"

"Mama, this is Isaac, you know my friend Gloria? This is her younger brother. He was one of my clients."

"Ah, ah. Omo mi, Gloria. Welcome, omo mi. How are you? How is work? How are your parents?"

Isaac, whose hands are folded behind his back, bends slightly in response to her greetings.

"Have you met the kids? Those naughty little things?"

He smiles, showing off his dimples. I notice Mama's brief frown, then nothing.

"No, Ma. I was here very briefly during the naming ceremony but I've been traveling ever since. Just got back to the country so I said, Let me just quickly stop by."

"Ah. Very good of you, my son. Thank you."

She looks around.

"And have you had anything to eat?" she asks.

He stares at me. I look away. "Oh no, Ma. I'm not hungry. I just ate. I'm coming from a wedding."

"Rara o. Nothing like that. Arin will quickly make jollof rice for you."

I bite my tongue.

"Come to the parlor, come and look at them."

He looks back at me as they leave. His eyes brim with tears I don't understand. He is smiling, though, and that's all that matters. My chest feels clogged, too, sad about something I cannot explain. I feel like I'm outside my body, watching this happen to someone else. As I work, smells come too sharply: of curry, and of chicken soaked in water, of my breast milk staining my dress, of him. The sounds are the same. His laughter is broken cackles, stored in the walls. Hers is soft and colorful. She tells him the twins are responsive and warm toward him because they can tell he is related to Gloria. If only she knew.

I occasionally walk into the parlor to see him kiss their faces or throw them up into the air. He can tell them apart. Their resemblance grows in front of me. Before it was just the dimples; now it's the nose, flat and fat at the nostrils, the birthmark in the bridge between their eyes above the nose, the elf ears. My chest is clogged, there are tears sitting at the bottom of my throat.

When he starts to leave, the babies cry. I tell him they're only being dramatic, like me. He slips a crumpled paper into my hand. I read it late at night when Hakeem is spooned against me, his eyes closed.

Thank you for bringing them into the world for me. Eternally indebted to you.

The news comes on a dry Friday night. It is Christmas Eve. Hakeem is cooking dinner while Hussain sucks from my breast. Hassan is in his cot in the nursery. The room smells of palm oil sizzling in a pot. I take Hassan outside to the veranda until it dies down. When we return, the fluorescent bulbs are on and the table is set. I rock Hassan to sleep, singing, "My Hassan, my sugar, let me love you forever, oh yeah" into his ears until his giggles trail off.

The tiles are white and dusty, and I imagine myself crawling on their coolness and inscribing Isaac's name in cursive into the grime. It's been three days since he was here. Mama has returned home to Ilorin, where she'll spend the holiday with Baba and some of her other grandchildren. Hakeem drove her to the park this morning. There was something flat on her tongue when she hugged me goodbye. I saw it in her eyes when she pulled me back and told me to call her anytime I needed her.

My phone rings from the kitchen.

"Sugar," Hakeem calls out for me, "Gloria is calling."

I taste the beans before I walk into the kitchen. They burn my tongue.

He's just picked up the call and is asking how she is.

"She's here," he says and hands me the phone.

"Glory, hallelujah!" I say.

She laughs a little.

She asks me to put the phone on speaker. Hakeem turns on the faucet and washes his hands.

"You guys, I have bad news," she says.

"Hmm?"

"I don't know how to say this."

"What the hell is going on, G? Are you sick? Is something wrong with your mum? Please talk."

Hakeem motions for me to calm down. He runs slender fingers into my hair. I try not to look irritated.

"I've been putting off this call because I thought I'd be in Nigeria for Christmas." She sighs. I can picture her eyes, the small, round honey balls in a pool of white, and the wells in her neck as she searches for words. Her voice is thin and slippery when she finally says: "Isaac is dead."

The phone slips out of my hand. Hakeem catches it before it reaches the tiles.

"Did you say Isaac is dead?"

"Which Isaac?"

"What are you talking about?"

"When? How?"

Hakeem and I are talking at the same time. I'm not sure whose words belong to whom.

"He died four weeks ago, November 24. He slept and didn't wake up. He was buried this Tuesday."

My lips tremble. This Tuesday? But he was here. He came by on Tuesday. I saw him.

*   *   *

The churches are singing and praying and I can hear them like they're here trying to exorcise my demons, here in this room where the sky spins and the ceiling cannot hit the floor without breaking me. It's New Year's Eve and I'm in this hotel on the island, far from home but not too far. I've been in the tub for four hours now. The scented candles make me fall asleep, but only short naps at a time. I dream inside each nap. Some of the dreams are memories, most are of Isaac, some are of Hassan and Hussain. In my dreams of the twins, their faces merge into each other to become Isaac's and they die. In my dreams of Isaac, I see him at the nail salon the day we first met. I watch as love oozes out of his skin and into mine when we shake well-manicured fingers together. In another, we have sex on that last day, when he was already dead. We are sweaty and moaning in front of Mama and the twins.

Each time the soft knock of room service comes, I tell them to go away.

My phone is dead now. Before it died, it rang almost every minute. At least I'm taking baths now. In the past few days, all I've done is sit at the window seat and look at the busy roads. I wondered what it would be like to jump these nine floors, crack my skull and spill my brains.

I'm never returning home. What's the point of living, of continuing to see what I can now confirm are Isaac's children—no paternity tests needed, because a mother knows these things—and be reminded that he no longer exists? I told Hakeem after Gloria's call, blurted it and watched his face turn pale until it stopped and melted into softness. He didn't care that they were not his children. He held my shoulder instead and said, "They're my children." What did I do to deserve a rare man like him?

The bottle of wine on the edge of the tub falls and breaks when I try to get out. I hold things to steady myself but end up stepping on glass and bleeding.

I ignore the pain and plug in my phone. When it comes on, I find several texts from Mama, telling me it's okay to mourn but that my kids need me. Oko mi, she starts all her texts. I wonder how she's not shaken when she experienced the same thing, a dead man's coming.

A dead man came to me. Touched my skin. I felt his erection. He was real. I pull at my hair, confused.

There's no one to share the physical pain of this loss with. Gloria is not here but her texts are full of light and love. Hakeem is worried. He texts, "Sugar, come home, I love you." How does he still want me?

January skies hover and carry a mixture of hot and cool air that makes between my toes and inside my palms moist. It's been ten days since New Year's Eve; several suns have come and gone but it's my first day out in one.

My skin was crawling and my scalp was burning when I called Hakeem this morning to tell him I needed to return home. He arrived in no time, and we went to the salon together to shave my head bald. Now he drives to the pharmacy; the nausea can come anytime. I know what it is, as I knew the first time. I don't need the tenderness and vomiting to know a person as tiny as a feeling sits in me. It is confirmed when a bird flies in front of us, smiles for only a brief moment before it flies away.

I ask Eledumare to bring Isaac back. I silently pray for this baby to be Babajide, a reincarnation of the father of the twins, a reincarnation of one of my best friends, Isaac. Isaac. I stare at Hakeem, at his kind eyes and overgrown beard. I hope he'll understand what's coming, and understand my love for this new child. I want to hug him, to nestle his face between my breasts. I can't, he understands. I cheated on him, yet I behave like he's the one who needs forgiveness. His left hand is on the steering wheel; his right hand is on my thigh. He parks in front of the pharmacy and starts to get out, when I tug at his sweater.

"Hakeem," I say. "This one is all yours." I place my right hand over my flat belly.

"I know," he says. "We'll call him Babajide when he comes." He smiles but I don't think of the forgiveness inside his eyes. I think of that first bird that came the morning after, that bird that winked, and told me with honesty in its orange eyes everything I could not see.

UNTIL IT DOESN'T

by ROY UDEH-UBAKA

If you must read this story, here is how you must read it:

J: as a boy, soft-spoken, prim; as a man, the same
K: your typical boy, craggy, gentle when he needs to be; as a man,
different
We: everything that exists within and between them

IT'S 1972, AND THEY are fifteen. Here is where we meet them: J is at the entrance to the library, stuffing a book into his backpack. K is across the street, plucking at a dried-up tree. K turns and sees J, waves him over, calling his name. J notices his stained blue trousers and his unkempt hair, arches a brow. He crosses the street and reaches for K, runs a hand through the stubble on

K's cheek and moves it up to his head. K doesn't smile at first, merely stares at him. Then he does, the same smile from his eyes. It's a cold harmattan day, the empty street lined with shriveled trees and dust-patched houses, and we know where we are. This is the beginning of a love story.

There is a tale long told, about a boy and a girl, and a love so desper-ate it snuffs the life out of them. This may not be the version of the tale you are familiar with, but this is the version we are telling. For the sake of this story, let's tell a part of it from J's shoulders.

Time has flickered by. A year, then two. He's beside K as they walk into the church. This is the first time they have been to a church in years. K's grandmother has died, and everyone is present. They find a spot in the second pew. K sits beside his mother and sister, and J curls up beside him. He has brought a book, a light one, in case he gets bored. Something to fan himself with, he tells K when asked. They do not say anything for a while, just listen to the reverend talk, about how beautiful a life the woman lived, how treasured she was. An aunt at the other end of the church bursts into tears, and J is immediately amused by it. He is sure K is, too, but he doesn't show it. We have no memory of the first time they met—we weren't there—but it was in the school canteen, they've said, two boys, out of place in a crowded school. It was a year before we met them, maybe two; we don't know—we weren't there. But something about being in this church conjures the image of it. He wants to tell K now that he is ready to use the *l* word. K used it the day his grandmother died, and in the months leading to the funeral he's become sure he's ready. The church is dense, and there are sounds of muffled crying somewhere. On the bench, he runs his fingers into K's, and they remain this way, their bodies rising and kneeling in supplication, fingers locked. Outside, the weather is clear and bright, and we know he won't say the words.

Rain splatters on the windows of K's father's station wagon, and the heat from their bodies rises and fogs up the glass. They are parked a few blocks from J's house, headlights dimmed. Fela's "Gentleman" comes on the radio, and they sing along to it. Several times they have done this. Several times we have watched them sit in the dark in K's father's car, singing along to songs from the radio and sipping beer from paper cups. But today something is different: J wants him; we know this. It's in his eyes, the way they linger on K's body, the slant of his shoulders, the small of his neck. K is so beautiful he has to remind himself to breathe. Bare feet against the dashboard, J exposes the smooth thinness of his legs. K runs a finger across his thigh in the shape of a heart, and J repeats the pattern on the foggy window. They don't say anything for a while, and we are not sure what J will do until he does it. He reclines the passenger seat and pulls his shorts down to his knees. He says, I want you, and brings K's hand to the center of his legs. He is aroused by K's nervousness, and he smiles and assures him that it's all right. He unbuttons K's shirt and runs his hand across his skin, twirling his fingers atop his nipples. The dark hair on K's chest is more than he'd imagined, and he's surprised by how little he knows of his body. K is hard and hot and smells like mint, and when J takes him in his mouth, K grips his head and thrusts deeper. We look away. Later, his skin smells of K, and he inhales it until it doesn't.

*   *   *

No one ever comes here; no one reads the sun-bleached posters on the walls and electrical poles that line the narrow entrance. We can tell because there are no littered beer bottles and cigarette butts lying around. Here: a make-shift beach on the outskirts of town overlooking the stream. It looks like you would expect—desolate. Abandoned to its devices. The water is barely knee-deep and does not quite flow like an ocean. But if we listen carefully, we can hear the waves roaring. J has the entire afternoon planned out. He arranges a mat by the sandy shore and unpacks a basket of sliced apples and drinks and toasts. K watches as he smears jam on the bread, sipping from a bottle of beer. When they are done, J runs off, nimbly stepping on the hot earth. K is slower, behind him, less sure-footed, bending to pick up a rock. When he looks up, J's far away at the other end, across the water. They run and play and get sand in their hair. The week before, K turned eighteen, and there was a party at his house. J recalls it now, K in a green suit and a red brooch, all man and set for the world. There is a posed photo of them. No one sees this, but in it their hands are touching, however lightly, they are touching. He wonders, now, if K remembers it, their hands touching. He wants to ask but doesn't. They watch the big orange sun on the move; quietly, as though savoring the moment, they watch it get closer and closer to the dark side. Their eyes are full of laughter, their smiles wide. From a distance, we, too, watch and smile and cry a little, and we wish we could stay with them in this moment forever.

He leaves tomorrow. He wants a fresh start, a new beginning of his own. We understand this desire. We, too, want to be free, yet we wish this wouldn't happen. A scholarship in Bristol, he tells K. K, on the other hand, will be studying engineering in Nsukka. They are at K's house, and nothing else seems to matter right now, not the distance, not what this distance could mean for them, and certainly not our continued existence. K brings him to his tidy bedroom in the old, creaky house. His parents are gone for the afternoon, taking a trip into the city. He wraps his legs around K's waist and his arms around his neck. K is so familiar to him now. The birthmark above his eyebrow. The thin lines of his lips. The hairs on his chest and calves. And then into his ear, he tells him. His tongue glazing it gently, he tells him. The words sink between them, and K glides into him slowly, then quickly, then slowly again, till he begins to scream the words more frequently. He knows that K has waited so long to hear them, and for a while, their desires match, and everything seems like the beginning of a new phase. But he leaves tomorrow. He wants a fresh start, a new beginning of his own. He wants to tell K this, but he doesn't. The distance will handle it.

There is a story they tell about leaving… No, let's not tell it here.
What you must know is that they left, so we left, but they are here and
so are we.

When we see J, he is in his apartment looking through the window at the sea. Lagos is the most beautiful in July. He leaves his window open, even in the rain; he enjoys the sound of the sea as it returns to itself. He is staring out at the far end, where the sun and the sea collide, inhaling the morning breeze. The evening before, someone told him that K is here, in Lagos, doing some business at the Atlantic. How long has it been? Eight years? No, ten. What has he been up to? He has heard many stories: some he believes; most he doesn't. His boyfriend stretches on the bed and he is snatched back from his thoughts. The boyfriend is awake now and is staring at him, willing him back to bed.

He walks to the bed, presses his lips against the boy's, and leaves to start the morning smoothie. He blends the fruits slowly, hoping the sound will cloud his thoughts. It's unlikely they will run into each other; somewhere within him, he hopes they do. We followed the letters that slowly stopped coming, trailed the telephone calls that soon went cold, the emails left unreturned. K is probably with someone else now, he tells himself. Ten years is a long time to stay stuck on one person.

When we see K, the television is muted in his room. The reflection from it helps him focus. He's staring, but isn't watching. His thoughts are scrambled. He heard J moved to Lagos after his university education. He doesn't want to run into him. He is glad to have moved on. He has a girlfriend, a stable life, a dog; things have been pretty fair with him. He falls asleep on the sofa, thinking and not thinking about him. He's still asleep when his girlfriend calls from a landline. Her voice is tender. She wants to know how he's doing, if he has eaten. Pressing the phone to his ear, he tells her that everything is fine; he's doing some research for his project. He reassures her of his love for her, and the line goes dead. He heats his dinner in the microwave and turns up the volume on the television set. A vibrant population, they say, and he knows J is part of it—somewhere—inhabiting, reassuring someone else of his love.

J is taking his usual evening stroll along the beach; the wind is tender on his skin. He has on a straw hat and a loose-fitting shirt over a pair of orange shorts. His sandals dangle from his left hand. He likes the feel of sand between his toes. Under a tall coconut tree, he sees him, in a white shirt and gray shorts.

In what feels like a minute but could actually be a few seconds, their eyes meet, and J puts his hand up to wave. In the distance, the sun is setting, and the figure under the coconut tree looks away. The smile on his face thins out and is replaced with shame. Grateful for his hat, he turns and traces his steps back, trapping sand between his toes, digging his feet into the warm earth. Later, he's not sure if it was K after all.

By the entrance to a movie theater, he sees J, standing with a man in a well-tailored suit. He's laughing, hard, his head thrown back, his palm slapping against his thigh, just as he remembers. It is the laugh—the wave of it—that makes him look over. J is, now, just as he was then. He doesn't pay any attention to the man in the suit; his attention is fixed on J. He hides under the shade of a tree and stays there, watching. He is still the most pleasant-looking man he has ever seen, and twenty-nine seems to agree with him. His legs are as slim as he remembers; his hair is combed up in a medium 'fro. He can't help staring, and we wish J would turn and see him too. J looks at the watch on his wrist, and they walk into the cinema. He stares till he can't see him anymore, glad he never saw them touch, even shake hands. Maybe he's relieved things happened this way. Perhaps watching as he leaves again is the closure he needs.

K's wedding invitation is in his mail, and it has lain unopened for two days. He battles about the possible content and what it means for him—for them. In between clients, he rips through the brown paper and finds the invitation card inside. His sister had called and said they ran into each other. He's so grown now, she said. He will call his sister and ask about the girl. In his mind, he conjures an image: thin, skin as dark as coal, spineless. We like this image in his mind. He looks at the card again and runs his hand across his name. There is a note: Please, come. K has signed it off with his name. The wedding will be held in Enugu, at the same church where his grandmother's service was held. He wonders if K has been back there since the service, if he has found his faith, found God; if he remembers their hands locked together. He hasn't been back to Enugu since he left, ten years ago. His parents died in a car accident while he was abroad, and home isn't what it used to be anymore. Before he refolds the envelope and tucks it in a side drawer, he reads the note again, imagines the preciseness of his plea. He promises to make an attempt to attend. We hope he will, yet we bet he won't.

He's not really awake. His consciousness is buffering at best. The child is crying from the next room, and he can sense his wife shuffling out of the bed. He checks the clock by the nightstand; it's past 4 a.m. Sleep has been a luxury since she was born. Enugu is lifeless at this time. He walks into his study, switches on his computer, and tries to get some work done, but can't seem to. He decides to go for a run, something he hasn't done in a while. The weather is cold at first, then tepid, then lukewarm, and he pulls off his sweatshirt and wraps it around his waist. On the way, he passes J's parents' house, now vacant. He hasn't thought of him in a while. He had hoped to see him at the wedding. He looks up, instinctively, at his bedroom window above the driveway. He jogs on, promises to forget him. He's getting good at it. We hate that this is happening, but we can't help it.

*   *   *

It's been three years since he received the invitation to K's wedding, and he is honeymooning on a resort island in the Maldives. He is happy; at least we think he is. His wife is pregnant, and everything seems to have worked out after all. The palm trees are twirling. The island is littered with coconuts, and the ocean is as blue as the sky. It's so beautiful, and yet his eyes carry a tinge of sadness. We wonder if he misses K, if he is wondering what it would be like to be here with him. His wife sneaks up behind him and wraps her arms around him. He shuts his eyes for a second, then wraps an arm around her shoulders. She is pretty in the right shade of light, and we are not sure how we feel about her just yet. Their marriage is accidental. No: the pregnancy was accidental, the marriage customary. A product of a drunken one-night stand. But he's happy; at least we think he is.

The wind is dull, the air carries a sense of mourning, and it's the day of his father's wake. The house is filled with strangers muttering the same platitudes. K isn't prepared for the gathering of well-wishers and strangers telling him he will be all right. His wife takes the girls—five and two now—back to the house; they aren't used to seeing him so disoriented. He's hugging someone and he looks to the next person and there he is. He cries then, with his arms wrapped around J, his head against his shoulder. He cries like this until everyone has left. They spend the night in J's hotel room, cuddled up under the sheets, saying nothing, just holding each other. We are alive again in this moment; our tongues thirst for what this could mean. Hunger for more. Reach, with every touch, for a little more, just a little more. He is gone before J wakes, and he wishes he had left a note.

*   *   *

Let's tell that story of the lying boy. Whenever his mother sends him on an errand, he spends several hours playing with friends and comes home with stories of different creatures he had to battle on his way home. One day, he goes off into the forest to fetch some firewood for his mother. There, he meets an old woman who asks him to help her lift her bundle of firewood onto her head. I am sorry, old woman, he says. Last night, I slept on my palm and twisted it terribly. I can barely move a muscle. She looks at his hand, in which he holds an ax, but doesn't see where he claims he is hurt. If that is what you wish for yourself, the old woman says, I wish you the same. He walks away whistling and sets off to fetch his firewood. Wielding the ax, he dislocates his arm and lies there in the forest screaming and squealing with pain, but nobody hears him. When his mother comes in search of him later in the night, she finds his body, stretched out on the dry weeds, his right arm impossibly twisted.

The moral of this story, perhaps, is that lying can kill you, slowly but surely. Or perhaps the moral is that old women can curse you, or that lying to old women can get you killed. Or perhaps it is that lying is just another way of guarding the truth. The truth will set you free, they say. We know a handful who have died from following this.

In his sitting room back in Lagos, J is seated across from his wife and the twins as she plays with them. His mind is a maze and he tries to focus on the things before him. He picks the babies up one after the other—boy, then girl—and twirls them in the air. They squeal and make babbling sounds, laughing. He is trying not to think about that night in Enugu, how much he had wanted to do, to say. How much of their lives were shed on the floor as they climbed into bed. He thinks about the morning after, waking up to an empty room that still smelled of K. He remembers the anger he felt, yet he's glad it happened the way it did. He cautions himself to spend more time with his family. The next weekend he takes them to the zoo. The twins are too young to make out the animals, but they babble along with them, hopping around in his arms.

For the past two years, since his father's funeral, he has expected a call from J. He has started to send an email and stopped himself, written letters he's torn into tiny pieces and flushed down the toilet. They are in bed now, he and his wife. Her head is pressed against his right arm, and he strokes her hair lightly. She's still as beautiful as the first day he saw her. He still reassures her of his love each day. It's in the little things: the flowers he buys, the birthdays he never forgets, the anniversaries he shows up for, the kisses on the lips before he leaves for work. There are three kids now, and she's pregnant with the fourth. He didn't want this child, but he smiled when she told him. Another baby, he said. I'm sure we can handle it. The next morning, he takes his family to the amusement park. They sit in the Ferris wheel, and the kids scream at the top of their lungs when it gets to the top. They eat ice cream from a cone and it drips all over their hands and shoes.

It is important to this story to know that J never has any more children. The twins are five, and they argue so much now. His wife wants more children; he is sated with just the two. Here is the thing about their marriage: she pushes, and he pulls back. It's the morning after their sixth anniversary and he is up early, getting ready for the day. The night before, he had walked into their bedroom, where she was lying on the bed, her red thong blooming. Slats of light curved over her body from the bedside lamp. She wore pale pink eye shadow; her hair was resting against the pillow, her eyes closed, the lids fluttering. He had stared at the scene for a few seconds and pulled the blanket up to cover her nakedness before walking into the bathroom. In there, he took the pills, one, then two, and hoped it would work this time. He craved alcohol, but he knew she would smell it on his breath. He popped a third pill, reading the prescription in his mind: two tablets per dose. He waited thirty minutes, brushing his teeth and running warm water in the tub. There is a boy, though, young, dark, and faintly broad. In the right shade of light, his eyes are K's. He has a tender smile, and we like that this makes J smile too. With him, J never has to take the pills. Their arrangement is physical: they have sex, and J pays him. The third pill kicked in. Drowsy from the side effects, he splashed running water on his face and walked back into the bedroom; her eyelids were still fluttering. He pulled down the blanket and ran his hand across her bare butt. There was a smell of something sweet as she pulled him close to her. She wrapped her legs around his waist and he slipped, now erect, into her. While they made love, he touched her face and said, You're so beautiful, and she gripped his back firmly, jerking her waist forward and back. Afterward, he spent an hour in the shower scrubbing his skin. She had fallen asleep by the time he was done in the shower, and she is asleep now as he leaves for work with a kiss on her forehead.

K follows the news every day, watches on his television as gunshots are dispersed into the air, rings of black smoke rising to the clouds from burning houses and car tires, people running from one street to another. There is no news of whom the country is at the mercy of, and everyone is law. His wife's cousins visit from Lagos and they share the guest room downstairs. In the sitting room, they talk about Lagos, and how the media covers only a third of what actually happens there. They talk about the families burned alive along major roads, and the houses set on fire with their occupants still in them. From the directory in his office, he dials J's office number and his secretary answers. He doesn't leave a message or a name. He promises to call back. He gnaws at his cuticles till they form little globes of blood. He is not sure what he is waiting for, but he waits. By the phone, he waits.

A misplaced bullet cracks through his bedroom window in Lagos, and he is back in his father's house in Enugu. His sister gave him the keys, and the house smells of insecticide and mothballs. He plays *Zombie* on his father's old record player, and he finds that he still remembers the words. That night, his son has an asthma attack, and they spend their first two nights at the hospital where his parents died. Daddy, where is Mummy? his son asks when he wakes up, and he holds him close to his chest and assures him that his mother will be back. Silently, he hopes she will. They'd had a big fight about moving to Enugu. She'd wanted to stay. He needed to leave. There is no one there, she said. It's what's best for everyone, he said. I will go to my parents' place for a few days, she said. I will meet you in Enugu. He had looked at the face of his wife, the beginning and end of her resolve both etched there. They slept on opposite sides of the bed, and in the morning, as she packed two bags and set off with their daughter, he shut his eyes, unable to move, and assured himself that she would come back. She doesn't say it when he calls her about their son, but we know she blames him for the asthma, for everything.

*   *   *

His daughters are grown and do not smell like babies anymore—milky sweetness replaced with something harsh and delicate, like roses, lilies. The boys are in senior secondary. And their mother is ill. Cancer has laid siege to her lungs and threatens to drain the life out of her. They spend most of their days in the hospital with her. She is strapped to an IV, and her face is sunken. The veins on her arms and feet pop out in varying lines. He is holding her hand when the first call comes. It rings twice again before he steps out to take the call. Hello, the caller says. J's voice is still as calm as he remembers. He leans against the wall and shuts his eyes, inhales with a sigh of relief. The conversation is awkward at first until J mentions that he is in Enugu. Neither attempts to divulge any deeper information, and the call ends in a formal tone, with a willingness to get together sometime for a drink. The millennium comes, and sometime never does. They run into each other at First Bank, a week before J is to move back to Lagos, and they shake hands and hug, sad about the unbridged distance between them since he's been back. J asks about his wife, and he frowns and shakes his head. They plan to get drinks later that night, shake hands, and hug again. K spends the night at home with his wife, and by morning, we are miles apart again.

His daughter visits before she goes off to the university. She lives in Lekki with her mother, who he heard has remarried. There was no invitation, and they rarely talk about her new marriage. They endure conversations about the twins: their schooling, scheduled vacations with each parent, his disapproval of her decision to change their daughter's last name. His daughter sits across

186

the room from him. She's much grown now and her face is her mother's. She wears a wig and has kohl under her eyes. She doesn't say much; she responds in monosyllables. The year before, his son began to court a girl in his school who has a warm smile and a bright presence. They are off to the same university in Ibadan, the three of them, and we are sure things will work out fine. The twins have a relationship that excludes him and his ex-wife, and for this he is grateful. He wants to ask if she is seeing anyone, if her mother lets her experience things in her own way. I'm so proud of you, he says to her, and she looks up at him and smiles. It is not a lot, but he will take it. When she leaves, he reaches for his mobile phone, scrolls down to where K's number is saved. He stares at the device for a while, and we are tempted to push the DIAL button.

Death is waters he has learned to wade in. On a cold harmattan morning, the cancer takes the last chunk from her lungs, and his wife dies. The bed in the old, creaky house squeaks beneath her weight, and he knows she's dead before he feels her pulse. He does not cry. He does not let go. He holds her palm, rubbing and rubbing it between his, determined to keep a part of her warm. He stays this way till late in the evening, when the ambulance he called comes to take her. He does not let go. He continues to rub her palm until she is pried away from him. Only then does he cry, leaning against the entrance to the mortuary, his face in his hands.

There is a story to tell here, but we do not remember it. What we know is that it is a story about loss, about a boy who swims through seven rivers and climbs seven mountains, only to get to the end of his journey and die from a scorpion's sting.

J doesn't attend the funeral service. The old, creaky house has been repainted. He doesn't remember what color it was, but he is sure it was not the shade of white it is now. A banner with a photo of K's wife stretches from the top left of the house to the ground. They have chosen a good photo. She is just as he'd imagined her: thin, skin as dark as coal, spineless. What he hadn't imagined was how beautiful she was, the gentle calmness of her eyes, lips that seemed to quiver, however lightly—how much their first daughter replicates her. By the entrance to the house, she stands by her father, welcoming guests. K smiles and shakes hands with the guests. Clearly, she is beside him for support. He's somewhat slanted, like an invisible part of him rests on her shoulder. For a while, J watches this sight from one of the canopies in the compound, before approaching to shake hands with K. He wonders what the introduction will sound like: *Meet my childhood friend, Mr. So-and-so,* or something in that light. He wonders if he has told them about him, or if, like for him, the life they shared has remained between them, tucked somewhere deep and unsullied. There is no introduction. K hugs him, pats him on the back twice, and thanks him for coming. He leaves thinking and not thinking about a proper introduction. It irks him that there was no introduction, but he doesn't admit it to himself.

It is 2017, and they are sixty. Nearly five years have passed since the funeral, and neither seems to recall the awkwardness of it. They exchange emails about their children and the influence of social media on the recent generation. Together, they catch up on abbreviations. What is "LMFAO"? J asks him. Do you understand this meme? K asks. Their children are working and have followed paths of their own. K's boys are in grad school abroad. They sign each email with tender words: *Love, Dearest, Yours*. K doesn't understand emojis just yet and reads in them the funniest meanings. We like this. We are alive again. The year before, J retired from his practice and moved back to Enugu. He lives in his father's house with his sister, whose husband has died. We should get that drink, J said in his last email, and they agree to meet at a bar in New Haven. J is early. He sits at the far end of the bar and gulps down a glass of Heineken to calm his nerves. He wants to look busy when K shows up, so he opens Jeffrey Archer's *Kane and Abel* and pretends he is reading it. He feels like "smart" is his most attractive look. They hug an awkward hug, a few hand pats on the back, and we wonder if by the end of the date the hug will be tighter. K orders a bottle of Guinness and sits beside him. They are self-conscious and they interrupt each other.

There is something appealing and beckoning outside, something that reminds us of new beginnings. We look away for a second at the couple across the street from the bar, and the air is different when we return. J argues that K's views are conservative. K says that schooling abroad has made him forget the cultures of our country. There is a cold silence between the two, and we are not sure exactly what it is we missed. They sip their drinks quietly. J checks his wristwatch. K taps at the keypad of his phone. We chide ourselves for looking away. We should have been here, watched them closely. We should have seen it happen. There is hurt somewhere, but we do not allow it to linger. The door closes behind us and we are beside the couple across the street as they lock hands. The boy (we should call him F) holds the girl (well, D) to his chest and he inhales the smell of lavender in her hair. The weather is damp, and there is a feel of rain ahead. We take a final look back inside the bar, and neither even realizes that we are gone.

BECOMING
THE BABY GIRL

by ADACHIOMA EZEANO

I. ME AND MUSCLED MAN

IT'S EXAM. TALL THIN girls don't show up. I wonder if they are all all right. I ask the course rep where they are. He's busy re-reading his worn-out, photocopied version of Iweka's *Introduction to Drama*. He doesn't even look at me. I sigh. Prof. Okafor comes in with muscled men. They come with guns and anger. They come with swearwords. They stand us up. They search us. The taller one searches me. He touches my breasts and my eyes bulge. My mouth forms a *whaat?* He says, "Why is it hard?" He asks, "Do you have expo there?" "No, I don't bring prohibited reading materials into the exam hall," I say. "You can," he says. "I don't see why you should not," he keeps on saying. "Everybody does it. Only, they have protectors. I will be your protector. Give me your phone number and yourself." I hiss. I call him idiot. I call him useless.

I call him stupid. I call him a very, very useless man. My voice ascends with each word. He screams at me to shut up. He turns to Prof. Okafor, tells Prof. Okafor, "This girl carry expo oo."

"That's a lie! That's a lie!"

"Fill out the examination malpractice form, first of all," Prof. Okafor says to me.

"Why would I do that? This guy is just lyi—"

"No, no, you will not call this honorable man a liar. Fill this form out, young lady. Fill it!"

I take the malpractice form from where he piled them on the table, write my name, and wonder, Can they do this to tall thin girls? Tall thin girls wearing power as perfume and flipping long, dangling braids or costly wigs, brandishing beauty and snobbery like they are the only humans in this universe. This muscled man and this professor. Can they do this to tall thin girls?

2 . ME ON MY FIRST DAYS HERE

I sway my hips past people with my lips slightly parted. I walk past people with grins on their faces, past people with inquisitive looks and no shame as they say, "Hey, fine girl." I say to them with determination that I'm not here to be fine girl and agree with myself: I am not here to be fine girl. I braid my hair in a Ghana weave with black Darling attachments, wear the long skirt Dad bought with the oversize shirt Mum bought. Both of them wiped tears with white handkerchiefs when I pulled out my traveling box. I left them behind with our thin yellow dog, Jack. Jack, with his pendant ears. I wear my mother's cat's-eyes and my pointed nose that everyone believes my father made possible. Dad fills me up with *don't forget* advice as he drives me to Lagos Park: "Don't forget where you come from." "Don't forget where you're going to." "Don't forget to choose the right company." When my bus pulls away from Enugu, I try everything I can think of to connect where I'm going with where I come from. When I dab my face with the white handkerchief Dad gave me before he swerved off in his car to go home, it is tears I wipe from my eyes. I hope never to forget.

3. I CAN'T BE TALL THIN GIRLS

Three tall thin girls who are colored like sun, who burn through the class, who let out loud clangs of laughter, who put on airs like they are Beyoncé, who say, "Yeah, you guys, what the fuck, yeah, yeah," who wear English like it is a song, who come to class in too few clothes, clothes that look like they'd fit a two-year-old, who wear long hair extensions worth as much as my father's bungalow, who wave their hands and their perfumes waft around and take over the class. These tall thin girls, who are liked by all the boys and all the men in this school, who bad-mouth Prof. Chris and boo Prof. Okafor, who make girls wish to be them. Those tall thin girls who call to me on the Monday of the first week I walk into this new school and say, "That forehead, oh my god, you look like you are Rihanna right now." Those tall thin girls who call to me on the Tuesday of the second week I walk into this new school and say, "Your shirt, girl, your shirt. Mehn, it looks damn so good, really, giirrl." I wear the loose-fitting white shirt Mum bought from her neighbor who sells imported secondhand wears. Those tall thin girls who call to me on the Thursday of the third week I walk into this school. They say, "Your hair, is that natural? The way it falls straight like a river, really, is it natural?" My hair has drunk uncountable cups of cheap relaxer. My hair doesn't fall straight like a river. My hair is not natural.

Now, those compliments have consequences: the urge to constantly google Rihanna. Place her picture side by side with mine. Compare and contrast. The urge to reshape my loose shirts, make them tighter. Starch them. Buy new ones. The urge to cut my hair. Patiently regrow it till it falls like a river. The urge to become tall thin girls, beautiful, effortlessly confident, eager to dole out compliments.

Who wouldn't want to be tall thin girls? Tall thin girls who drive around the school in Venzas and Lexuses; tall thin girls who are gold; tall thin girls who are bold. But I like to think I am not cut out to become tall thin girls. I am the girl who remembers where she is from and where she is going, who chooses who she goes there with. That is what my father has always said to me, and I am the girl who is her father's daughter, so I ignore tall thin girls on the Friday of the fourth week when they say, "We like you. Be us."

Well, I do not completely ignore them. The tallest of them, the one with the face shaped like an egg, skin the color of Angelina Jolie's, looks at me and says, "Heyy, my name is Ella. Can I have your phone number, please?" And my mouth goes to work telling it to her.

4. ME AND THE MIRACLES TALL THIN GIRLS MAKE

Now it is tears I wipe from my face again. It is holiday, though I am not going home. I am waiting for the school's disciplinary committee on exam misconduct to sit. No one knows when they will, or if they will, and only when they sit will I know if I will be rusticated from here. For now, I do not know. The letter I received many days ago orders me not to travel yet, orders me to stay till my fate is stated. I don't live off campus—only the rich students do that—and the school hostel is closed by management, to be reopened when school resumes in a month's time. So for now, I put up at my friend's house, and don't know where I will go from here. She says she is going to the village to help her mother with farming and trading so they can save for her school fees next session. They will harvest crops and sell vegetables and yams in the open market. She hasn't gone yet. I beg her not to, not to go yet, not until I find somewhere to stay. I like to think she will give me her key when she leaves. She hasn't said so yet. I only hope, keep saying, "Shebi, you'll leave your key for me when leaving, right?" But a daughter not yet free from her mother's loins will wear her mother's pants. So I wasn't surprised when, two days later, the earliest sun not yet blinding the moon, she sprang from her side of the bed and hit my bare shoulders over and over till I stretched and said, "Ah-ah!"

Her mother had called, had said, "It's either I see you here now or you see me there now." So, a girl goes home. She shrugs. I ask for her key. She says nothing. I ask for her key. She says nothing. I ask for her key. She breaks into a story of a young girl like us who made millions last month, just like that. So I pack my stuff as she packs her stuff. I stand by the back door, watch her apply her makeup, rub red lipstick, pencil her brows, wipe off the red lipstick, apply a pink stick, use contour on her face and look extra good. I want to tell her she looks extra good, but I'm not sure I want to talk to her yet. I stand there, watch her drag her Echolac out with lips tightly shut, beads of sweat forming on her forehead, wrinkled lines appearing on her face to form a plea, begging me to help with the heavy box. I press my phone instead because I am not here to help if you are not here to help. Still I stand there, hoping she will say, *Here, take my key. Always lock my door o.*

"Come out, I need to lock the door o." I grab my handbag and drag my box out by Papa Okey's shop, where she and I stood last night, talking about the things I don't care to remember now. She drags her Echolac to the street, flags a bike, tells the rider, a man in a black jean jacket, that she is going to wherever. They bid whatever whatever price, and the man in the black jean jacket climbs down, helps her pull the Echolac up onto the bike, and they zoom off, leaving me in what I want to assume is an intentionally collected swirl of dust. A mild way of telling me to fuck off.

I stand there for hours, watching everything: hurrying men and women, girls and boys, strangers zapping off in my dream cars—Venza, RX 350, Porsche, Range Rover, honking cars and buses and motorcycles, bus drivers cursing one another while struggling for passengers; everything, indications of people busy and life fleeting. I stand there, by the side, doing nothing. My mum calls. I ignore it. I ignore it because ignoring is what you do when you know why a particular call is coming in and you know you have no answers yet to those variegated *wh-* questions you are destined to listen to while pressing that phone to your ear. Mum wants to know when I will be home. Who knows?

I lean my box against the peeling wall and walk into Papa Okey's shop, buy airtime, load the fifteen-digit pin into my phone, subscribe for a month's data, and open my WhatsApp. Maybe I can find someone I know who is still around, someone who could save me from sleeping on the street. Maybe. There are tons of new messages, from friends at home, course mates asking for this textbook or that, men who want, people who claim they care, then these messages from this I-don't-know-whose number. I check the profile picture. My eyes swell! It is Ella! Ella of the tall thin girls. Like, who in the class gets messaged by Ella?

MON., 2 MAR.

Hey Bby Gal 11:41 AM
Yeah..... Ella,, here 11:41 AM
Chat me up asaq. 11:50 AM
Asap** 11:51 AM

THU., 5 MAR.

Heyyy, 10:15 PM
Your ignoring my chats now or they are just not delivering? That's fucked up tbh 10:15 PM

This is Ella tho. Don't be a bitch, yeah? 10:15 PM

FRIDAY

Hey!!!!! 10:17 PM
You don't remember me or what? Gal. It's Ella. Ella! 10:27 PM
Audrey's friend. Queen's friend. Ella! Ella!!! 10:28 PM
Are you really ignoring my text 10:28 PM

YESTERDAY

Babes, 10:01 AM
I called you. You didn't pick. 10:01 AM

TODAY

Someone just told me the issue you had with Prof Okafor. 12:05 AM
Call me ASAP. We can help you deal. 12:05 AM

THIS SENDER IS NOT IN YOUR CONTACTS

BLOCK   **REPORT**

ADD TO CONTACTS

Ella! 10:20 AM
I just saw your profile picture now! 10:20 AM
Ella! Queen + Audrey's friend? 11:07 AM
Jesus Jesus! I am so oo sorry! Like how can I ignore you? 11:07 AM
I am so so sorry, ppleaad 11:07 AM
Please*** Biko 11:07 AM
I didn't have data,, haven't been here for ages now. 11:08 AM
Hello Ella, are you there? 11:08 AM

Heyy 6:06 PM
Sup with you and Prof Okafor? 6:06 PM

Eh! You heard? 6:06 PM

Lol Ofcoz I heard. Been meaning to reach U. 6:06 PM

Please, I beg you, help me with that man's issue o.
Please. I don't know any anyhow in this school. I cannot
afford to be rusticated or anything. biko 6:06 PM
Anyone** 6:06 PM

Where are you ATM? 6:07 PM

Papa Oks 6:07 PM
Papa Okey's** shop 6:07 PM

Kk 6:14 PM

You travelled? My battery is low. It shut down soon sef. 6:14 PM

Go and charge biko. 6:46 pm

Charge? No light here oo 6:46 PM
I don't even have a place to sleep 6:46 PM

Wot do u mean u dont hv place to sleep? 7:10 PM

I'll explain when we see 7:10 PM

Stay at that Papa Okey's shop. I'm driving down. 7:17 PM
Will call as soon as I am there 7:17 PM

OMG! OMG! ELLA!!! 7:17 PM

May God bless you eh. Thank youuu 7:17 PM

Ella? Are you here yet? 8:00 PM

Ella?? 8:17 PM

Ella??? 8:25 PM

I am at Papa Okey's shop 8:30 PM
I am parked where he sells kero. Where you dey? 8:30 PM
Are you there??? your phone off already??? 8:31 PM

MISSED VOICE CALL AT 8:32 PM

TAKE YOUR CALLS!! 8:33 PM

I see you. I see you. In brown Venza 8:33 PM

Yea. get in here. I didn't park well. 8:33 PM

I squint as I look into the night, partially blinded by the sparkly streetlights. I pull up my box and drag it to where she has parked. I am a little scared of these tall thin girls. She opens the passenger door for me to get in once I've pushed my box into the backseat. I resist asking for the name of her perfume that makes the inside of this Venza smell like it is a room in heaven. "Thank you very much, Ella. I don't know what I did right to deserve stressing you like this." She says nothing, nods and keeps bending toward her steering wheel, pressing her phone. It is an iPhone, those long, fine ones that are new and make you drool. We sit in silence. Well, more truthfully, I sit in silence. She is on her phone, pressing, exhaling now and then, smiling mild smiles. I stay quiet, don't know how to be next, yet.

Ella coughs before she says, "So where... do... we go from here, yeah?" This is our very first real conversation and right now I feel her accent. It sounds like she learned from someone who learned from someone who learned from an Americanah, a complete been-to who thinks staying in America is all we have to do to become Jesus.

"I dunno. I had..."

"Fuck it! My house. Where are your stuffs?"

"Oh, in the back here."

"By the way, your name is Akunne, right?"

My name is not Akunne. I don't say this. I don't tell her my name is Ofunne either. I only wait for her to buckle her seat belt before I begin to tell the story nobody asked of me. I tell of my temporary roommate, a.k.a. friend, who left me on the street. I tell of Prof. I tell of standing a whole day and watching the world pass.

"Wow," she says. I talk for close to thirty minutes. She says, "Wow." I say how honored I am to be helped by her, how grateful, how I deeply admire her and everything she stands for. She says, "Wow." I tell more because I do not want to sit and say nothing. I talk on: Whatever, whatever, yada, yada, Buhari Buhari. Prof. Okafor is worse than a corrupt president. You know, you know. EFCC should not only drag around politicians that misappropriate funds. Blah, blah. They should also handle humans who are mean to other humans. Or better still, there be a body for this. Yada, yada.

Ella just drives. No more *wows*. No nod. No *yeah*. No *fuck it*. But her silence sways me as much as she sways her head, which she does a lot, using her green-painted, long nails to brush her long, straight extensions from her face. But before she starts playing Davido's "Nwa Baby," she says, "Baby girl, you don't mind staying in my house, yeah? And yeah, the number I chatted you up with, yeah? Save it, yeah? And yeah, I hope you got sexy pictures on your profile, yeah? Because I want to see all them sexiness you got, yeah?" She swiftly sways her head, uses her green nails to push back her hair again before she winks at me. It looks like she's saying: *Welcome to being a god.* I am still wondering if I am ready for this.

5. ME AND TALL THIN GIRLS ARE *WE* NOW

We wear black dresses. We strut. We go to Prof. Okafor's office. Ella, Audrey, and Queen say I should stay in the hallway. It is nearly empty now, everyone still on break. A few weeks ago, students studded this place, strutting and carrying their files with pride because it is not easy to beat out a million candidates to secure a spot here. It doesn't matter whether that aunt or uncle of yours who knows a someone who knows a someone that collected something small, maybe money or kindness, worked it out for you, and now here you are, an undergraduate. No, it doesn't matter. We are here now, that's all. The future leaders of Nigeria.

Tall thin girls open the door to Prof.'s office. Audrey drags me into the room by my right hand, saying, "Come here, baby girl, come here." My eyes meet Prof.'s. He looks away immediately, says to Ella, "See to it that she writes fast, extraordinarily fast." He stands up from his chair, opens his cabinet, brings out the question papers, selects one, and gives it to me. He leaves his office. Ella takes out a textbook, throws it to me. "Use it. Don't waste my time, please."

"You know we will graduate top of our class, yeah?" Audrey says, smiles, pouts her mouth, winks at me.

"Leave her alone! She needs to concentrate," Queen says to Audrey.

"Is she writing with her ears?" Audrey says.

"You guys, don't be like that now!" Ella says and then turns to me. "Be fast."

I sigh, write and write and write. Or maybe, copy and copy and copy. Once I finish, we pile into Queen's ash-colored Lexus RX 330. I ask, "So do you know when the disciplinary committee will sit?"

They look at me, those three tall thin girls. They laugh. They say, "What the fuck, whaa? What the fuck…"

6. BECOMING THE TALLEST THINNEST

I wear new tongues now as well as say "yeah," "you guys," "what the fuck," "yeah, yeah," as well as sing English as well as slap the driver who brings me home as well as become Rihanna and Beyoncé and Cardi B as well as wear too few clothes and hair extensions costing the price of ten plots of land as well as empty bottles of skin-toning creams onto my skin till I shine shine like I am sun as well as drain expensive perfumes till people stop to ask how I got such a fine smell as well as become more beautiful than tall thin girls. Even their men say so. They choose me over them. It makes them happy, though, so long as I get picked and they get paid. They say, "This is why we selected you, because you blaze so bright and your brain burns like fire. We know. We always know the right ones."

7. BAD GIRL GONE GOOD GONE BAD

I lose it and stab my shadows when I hear my father's baritone blare over the phone. He calls more now, and when he is done asking how is school, how is class, how are you coping, my university daughter, he says, "Ofunne, be good. Be godly, okay? You will be home for the holiday this time around, right?"

When he calls, I hear him; when he ends the call, I hear him. I remember the last time I saw him, his hands on the steering wheel, his mouth telling me not to forget where I am from. Right now, I am wondering how a girl from where I am from did forget. I am thinking of all the men I have come to know over the past three months. Chief with the stomach like he swallows the continent for breakfast. He was my first. He was my very first because Ella says it brings good luck; having a wealthy man rip your hymen means you will never meet a poor man. Ever! I didn't tell her of Joshua, the boy living behind my new two-bedroom apartment who sneaks in after these chiefs have gone. He begs for tea and t-fare. I give him tea and t-fare and kiss and me. We moan together and I know that even if he had money, I wouldn't want him for that. Then there is Prof. Okafor. And the man with white beards. And the man who pays for the two-bedroom apartment. And this other guy, Igwe Obiora, who Ella made sure I'd never see again. All he gave me were multiple orgasms and cowries. He said the cowries were original, the original cowries my ancestors harvested human heads for. There are other men, too, people I work hard to forget. The only person I am working hard not to forget is me. I fear that in trying to be me, I missed, became tall thin girls instead.

I stand from my bed, go to church. I kneel. I say, "Heavenly father, forgive me, forget the things I did, accept me back." I skip classes. And when I don't, I sit far, far from tall thin girls. But they come. They knock and knock and knock and knock till I know I can't really dodge tall thin girls.

"Don't call me baby girl. My name is Ofunne." But tall thin girls don't care. They say, "Ofunne is bush, something the governor would not like to call you."

"Which governor?"

They tell me how the minister of education celebrated his birthday when I was idling out. They didn't call me, because I was idling out. They tell me the governor looked through Queen's phone while they gisted, chewed gum, and sipped rum. They tell me that among many pictures, it was my picture he saw and liked. They tell me he said, "Get this one for me na. Ha! See big ikebe! What, what will she cost me?" They tell me they are here to break my idling. When Ella says, "You are going to South Africa with him," I nod, forget my father in heaven, forget the one in Enugu, and say, "Please, call me baby girl once again."

8. IT'S JOHANNESBURG, BABY

So the governor calls my phone, calls me baby girl. So he says it this way: "beibei girl," like he lacks something in his mouth, teeth or tongue. When he first calls, I wonder which governor this is. I listen as he tells me, "Keep our relationship to yourself, just you should know it." I put everything he tells me in my mouth and swallow it with water. I prepare for the South Africa trip. I ride to the newest boutique in Lekki with tall thin girls. Once we've burned the money he sends for my prepping, we return so I can pack, and for the first time, tall thin girls don't look so glamorous, not more than me. I know they are jealous, not just because they say it and laugh but because I see it in their eyes. I sleep in Lagos today and know that tomorrow I will be sleeping in Johannesburg.

The governor calls. He says to me, "Beibei, we will not go to Johannesburg right now, but we will go very soon." He sends enough money to buy ten Venza cars. Tall thin girls say maybe he saw a thicker girl with a bigger ikebe, oh yeah. They laugh with their mouths wide enough to swallow a river. I want to tell them to get out of my flat, but my voice is too tiny to start a war. I say I want to go see my mum this weekend since the Johannesburg trip is off. Tall thin girls say, "For what?" We sit in my living room, quiet, wearing too few clothes, pressing our phones till Audrey reads out from a popular blog that there is a strike now. We google it and learn that the Academic Staff Union of Universities is negotiating higher salaries for lecturers, and they're meeting with governors. I smile. I say this is really why he postponed Johannesburg. Tall thin girls press their iPhones. I stand to turn on my AC; there is too much going on right now.

9. JOHANNESBURG, FOR REAL

10. PUKING OUT THE PARTY

The governor buys me a white Crosstour and says, "Keep this car. But keep us to yourself." And so I'm keeping the month we spent in Johannesburg after the strike ended to myself. I mean, I did not even tell tall thin girls what went down there, or else they would be minding me like I was a baby: "Have you taken pills, eh? How much did he give you, eh? Will you see him again, eh?" Well, now I am bigger, from all the dinners, I think, and I am back and yay, I have my own car, and the strike is off, and I am here at a very depressing party at Nkem's house. Nkem is the friend of Aboy, the senior special adviser to the minister of foreign duties. Aboy understands the real meaning of foreign duties. Apart from linking us up with the minister himself, Aboy has connections and gets me and tall thin girls influential men who reek of power and hard currencies and hardness. His ride or die babe, Nkem, is drama, and her house is for showing off, with her plasma TV and her washing machine and her Indian hair and her fake smile and her Aboy. I drink vodka and rum and run to the toilet because I retch, and then puke. I don't know why I puke, but I puke again. Nkem comes in to her toilet. I am facing the bowl and puking, and the bitch looks at me and says, "What the hell? You've got AIDS now? You slutting tall thin girls! What the hell. What the hell."

11. A DRUG AND A DRINK TO DRINK

It is exam. I am the only tall thin girl in the exam hall because I tell tall thin girls I want to write all my exams in the hall and not in the office so no lecturer will have the chance to grab my ass. Ella shrugs, says, "Your choice." Now I think I shouldn't have had such guts. It is a difficult exam. My hands shake and seem to be afraid of holding things. My pen won't stay put, keeps slipping through my fingers. In my head, there sit a million humans with hammers and they hit the hammers, and each hitting leaves my head thinner. I want to die, and that is the only feeling that comes close to describing it. That and the hollowness that hugs you only when you lose someone who you once breathed like the air. I lost myself, but I am not sure this is why I feel like I am holding hands with the butchered parts of my body. One of the invigilators taps me from behind, asks me, "Are you okay, dear?" Her voice is soft and patronizing. I am not a charity case and I do not know the best way to say *get lost* if not by handing in my blank papers to this thin woman. She collects them, walks to the end of the hall, and hands them over to the new professor, who doesn't know me and who doesn't know tall thin girls. I stand from my chair, hold the other students' gazes. I am used to holding the other students' gazes. I have become for many girls the star now. If they only knew what it's like. Like being a perfumed dead rat. I go to the table where an invigilator had earlier ordered we drop our bags and phones, grab mine, leave. It is an original Louis Vuitton Saintonge. The other tall thin girls would never keep a Louis Vuitton Saintonge, with its smooth calfskin and its soft tassels and its expensive price, on the same table where cheap secondhand bags cluster. Ella would have found handing over her bag a very valid reason to leave the exam. But not me, and this is one of the many things that worries Ella about me. I pull out my phone, an iPhone XS, dial my mother's number, walk to my car. When she says, "Hello, Ofunne m," I pause, exhale, say, "Hello, Mummy."

"Omalicha m, kedu? How was your exam? When are you coming home sef? Ha! It's going to a century since I saw you last o."

"Mummy, my exam, it was bad."

"How? What is the problem? Ogini?"

"I—I don't know. I don't know what I'm doing."

"What's the problem, nne'm?"

"Mummy, I don't know."

"Are you sick? Are you eating well?"

"I am tired, Mummy, very very."

I hear her exhale. She keeps quiet for some time. Then she asks again when I am coming home. I don't know if I am going home. I don't have plans of going home, but I say, "In two weeks' time, Mummy." And nod repeatedly when she asks, "I hope you are still prayerful eh?"

"I will be praying for you here, too, i nula? I will pray. Just have faith. Your exam will be okay."

"Okay, Ma."

"You will pass. Ah! Our king of kings. He's all-knowing, a miracle worker! Have faith, i nula?"

And I have faith. I have faith that the all-knowing king of kings will not make known to my mother the reason I am so tired, the reason I wasn't able to finish the test. He won't make known to her that I haven't stopped puking since Nkem's party; that when we hang up, I will drive straight to Ella's house for some drink she promised will stop my stomach from growing. Because the only thing I need to grow as a baby girl is my bank account, and maybe my breasts and, yeah, my ass. I don't actually think I'm pregnant. I took all measures. But I go to Ella's house because nobody tells Ella no.

Tall thin girls are splayed out on Ella's couch when I open her door that afternoon: Ella reading my worn-out copy of *Purple Hibiscus*, Audrey lying on the floor pressing her phone, Queen holding up a miniature mirror to her face. They want to know how my exam went. I am too tired to recount. Ella repeats, do I know my constant tiredness and headaches and constipations and swollen breasts and vomits and every other whatever can only be attributed to pregnancy? I roll my eyes. Earlier, when Ella said this, I ignored her, as I want to now. But she has a pregnancy test and as soon as I urinate into the brown cup she hands me and return it to her, she immerses the colored end of the strip into the cup. She pulls out the strip and we wait, her singing Ada's "I Testify" and laughing, me sweating and telling her, "Stop, stop, stop that song right now." And then she cackles, holding up the strip and pointing at the two colored lines.

"Oh, yes! Now drink this," she says, handing me a mug. "I will not have a pregnant baby girl."

I have faith that the all-knowing God will not show my mother this, either: me grabbing the mug, drinking the damn thing, wanting to vomit, the taste like rotten fish; me ignoring Ella as she says, "Don't even think about it" when I run past her to the toilet.

When I come out a minute later, Ella doesn't believe me that I didn't puke it up.

"Take this drug." I eye her. Look at Queen and Audrey to say something. Audrey speedily turns to her phone. Queen speedily turns to her phone. I sigh. I throw the drug into my mouth and drink my water. And I say to Ella, "Anything else?"

"No, my madam. Meanwhile, you left your small phone here yesterday o. See it on top of that table."

BECOMING THE BABY GIRL

"I did? Are you serious? I didn't even know to look for it. Ha!"

"Na so the exam do you? So, this is how bad this exam got to you eh?" Audrey says.

"Or is it the pregnancy?" Queen says, throws her head back and laughs.

Audrey says, "A number you saved as 'Gov' kept calling and calling, like he owns you for real. Is that the governor?"

"I thought you said you were no longer seeing the governor," Ella said.

"I am not seeing any governor. Give me my phone."

Audrey runs to the glassy center table, collects the phone, and puts it into her pocket. I sigh, walk to where she stands. She makes to walk farther, to make me chase her. But then suddenly she stops, pulls the phone out of her pocket, and begins pressing it.

"Give me my phone, Audrey. Ella, please talk to Audrey."

"Audrey, give the phone to her now now."

Audrey throws the phone at me. I dodge it and it hits the floor. The battery and the phone's back fall out. I pick them up, panting as I do so.

"I hope you're not hiding anything from us like this. Ella, see your babe o," Audrey says.

Ella looks at me and looks back at her book, which she is now pretending to read. I enter Ella's room, lock the door, sit there for a while. My mind runs around. I need to sleep, but I don't want to. I unlock the door, go to the living room, where tall thin girls are still lying around, grab my original Louis Vuitton Saintonge, pick up my car key, put on my slippers, open the door, and leave the house.

When I get into my car and lock my door, I dial the governor's number and listen to his campaign song till the governor says, "Hello." I do not let him start up with his usual boring "How thou art, my sugar, you know I love you, my sugar, blah blah, sugar, yada yada, sugar."

"I am pregnant," I say to him immediately, though I don't know why.

He keeps quiet for some time before he says, "You are supposed to be a secret. You are supposed to be secret, sugar."

I want to say I guess this sugar is too sweet to stay secret.

"Is he a boy?" he asks.

"I don't know yet na."

Nothing comes from him for a moment, and I wonder if the network is bad. But it's not. He sighs loudly.

"You are good, all right?" he says. I want to tell him about the drug and drink from Ella, but I worry that will worry him too much and he will worry Ella too much and Ella will worry me too much.

"Don't panic, sugar, tomorrow eh I will come. We will go and see the doctor together. I want a boy. You will remove the baby if the baby is not a boy, you hear?" I don't say anything. He repeats the question, asking, "You hear?" This time I say, "Till tomorrow, please."

He sighs, says he will talk to me later. I want to call my mother, tell her, but I know she will cry that her daughter has lost her faith, has brought dishonor to the family. I want to call my father, tell him, but I know he will sigh severely, say his daughter forgot where she comes from, brought dishonor to the family. I start my car, drive away from Ella's house. I want to go home, but I am not sure home is the two-bedroom apartment I can afford because my body houses an abundance of men. So I keep driving, and keep driving. And keep driving. And keep driving.

THE GOOD ONES
ARE NOT HERE

by CHUKWUEBUKA IBEH

There is a staircase close to the guards' quarters. It is lightly manned, and it descends to an underground tunnel from which you could find your way out. But you wouldn't do that, because no one who has ever attempted an escape has survived to tell the many stories of this place.

THE BELL RINGS JUST before morning, rattling the prison walls and jolting me into sudden wakefulness, so that I collide with Tee and involuntarily catch a whiff of her sour breath. She shifts and mumbles something incomprehensible. I wait for her snores to return before I lift her arm from around my neck with much more care than is necessary, pausing in midair when she stirs again, and then I place it beside her. All around, the other women in our quarters are spread out in various positions, their discontented snores too loud in the quiet of the night. A faint light filters in through the tiny window above, indicating that the moon is still there. It has to be at least three hours before daylight. There are footsteps receding down the corridor. I can hear the muffled whispers of the guards, speaking German. I can hear the fading echo of the bell in the brief stillness that settles thereafter.

I have not been dreaming. The bell has been rung. Somebody is dead.

"When a prisoner dies, the bell is rung to attract the attention of the undertakers. They'll move over to her quarters and remove the corpse. Then they'll take the body to the coffin room, along the corridor on the other end of the prison from the guards' quarters. The corpse will be laid inside a coffin and left there until evening, when one of them will nail the coffin shut and the other will assist him in taking the coffin to the burial place."

"Where's this place?"

"Not very far from here, but at least far enough to set you on your way without getting caught. If you are fast, of course. But you have to be fast. And you have to be even more careful. Do you understand?"

The corridor is an airless space without an end in sight. Its narrowness, coupled with the thick walls bearing faint markings only half-visible in the dim light, makes me feel claustrophobic. There is a tightness in my chest that makes breathing a labor. My toes ache from all that tiptoeing. On my bare feet, no one will hear me walk across the corridor, regardless, but my freedom is here, only a few hours away, and I do not have the luxury of chance. I think of Tee lying there, so gentle and oblivious, in her sleep. I wonder what she will think when she wakes up and finds I am gone. Will she tell the others I have finally joined the brave ones, and then go on surviving, waiting for my mauled, mutilated body to be returned and paraded by one of the guards, or will she be aware, in that intuitive manner of hers, that I have escaped alive, somehow? For the hundredth time, I weigh the risks of turning back to wake her and inform her of my plans. I stifle a sigh, defeated, shamefully aware that I never would.

"Tell this to a single soul and you can as well forget about leaving," the warder said all those months ago, and yet the memory comes to me, startling and vivid; his lips red and trembling, his fingers fumbling with his trousers' zipper, his expression sated.

I hear the footsteps before I see them, walking toward me with forceful purpose. It happens too quickly for me to comprehend. One moment I am alone, contemplating where to go, and the next, the light in the corridor comes on and I am ducking behind a wall, breathing my last prayers, certain I have been discovered. With eyes shut, I steel myself for what will follow, for the string of bad-tempered German slurs and agitated gestures, for the agonizing, heart-stopping minutes spent looking into the hard, unfeeling eyes of the superintendent. But a few moments pass and I have not been yanked by the arm and dragged along the floor to the superintendent's office. It takes a lot of courage to finally open my eyes and even more courage not to collapse at the sight before me. I am no longer in the corridor. In my blind wandering, I have ushered myself through one of the doors in the corridor into a different room. I am almost turning to leave when my eyes catch the sight of a structure in the darkness: a wooden boxlike structure. A coffin. I am in the coffin room.

There was soft tap on my shoulder. I looked up to see Tee.

"Tell me," she said.

"Tell you what?"

"What you're thinking."

"Hmm, nothing."

"Tell me about the nothing then?" she said, a smile already forming. It was a game that was ours, part of a routine born out of boredom: initiating monotonous conversations whose content we could already guess. At this point, always, we would both laugh and talk about something else, like the little ration of food we expected at dinner or the infectious-looking sores of the recent epidemic. But instead, Tee sat down on the floor beside me, making sure our shoulders touched. The silence between us was occasionally interrupted by the hushed voices of the other women.

"You're thinking of home," she said, finally.

"Aren't you?"

She stared at me for a while before she fumbled in her pocket for something and brought out a picture, which she handed over to me. It was old, marred with dust and grit so that I could only see the portrait in a blur. "That's my son. His name is Patrick."

"He's handsome," I said, feeling a little foolish. I wished I had known a little more about him, had known that she even had a son, a life, a story before arriving here.

She shook her head, her expression grave, as though disappointed that I had nothing more to say. "And wise. The night before I left Takoradi, he wouldn't sleep. He cried till morning. And then when I set out to leave, he stopped crying and stared at me with this blank expression that made my blood go cold." She smiled, bit her lip. "I didn't understand what that look meant then. I think I do now."

I reached out to hold her hand. She had never said so much in one breath before, had always kept the story of her life private even though she knew all of mine. I could tell from the sudden rasp in her breath that the little she had just shared had taken a toll on her. She squeezed my palm with a small smile, as though grateful I had not asked her to say more. She reminded me of Ijeoma, how particular she was about holding hands, that hopeful smile that had never left her eyes in the three years of being separated from her life as she had known it to be. And how I felt with her, not particularly regret, but a wistful sadness for what could have been.

Ijeoma had taken the talk of my trip lightly. I had not exactly planned to say anything—it had slipped out while we lay on her mattress, sated from lovemaking. I was leaving for Europe soon, I said, and she responded, laughing, that she was also leaving—for America. Because she seemed so confident that I was joking, and because it seemed she would not be able to see it any other way, I let it be in the meantime, bringing it up next a week from when I was due to leave for Lagos with Ma Brenda.

"Why does she want to help you?" she asked finally, after looking at the wall in silence for a long time.

"She runs a kind of NGO for girls. It's her way to empower them."

"You don't believe yourself, of course," she said, looking at me as though I had lost my mind.

"It would do the both of us a lot of good," I said. "I could find a job and send you money to move to a better place."

"This place has always served me well, Amaka; always served *us* well."

"I have to think of my mother, Ije."

"She agreed to this madness?"

"It's not madness." I thought of the crisp notes Ma Brenda had flashed before me, the quiet authority they exuded in her palms, and I knew Ijeoma would never understand. "I have to try."

She stared at me for a long time. "Your mind is made up," she said with a sad shake of her head.

"At a point, I considered bringing him with me," Tee said now.

"What? Bring who?" I could not remember exactly what she was talking about.

"Jesus. My son, of course! Who else?"

I stifled a sigh. I had briefly thought of bringing Ijeoma along, but an incredulous stare from her had silenced my suggestion and Ma Brenda had emphatically declined.

"Good thing you didn't," I said, and when she looked at me, eyebrows raised, I added, "I mean, look where he could have ended."

"No." She smiled again, shook her head slowly. "He wouldn't have made it this far. His journey would have ended on the coast."

I looked away. I was thinking as she was. All those girls shot as they tried to escape, after realizing the whole business of being transported to Europe to get jobs was a scam, after all. All those bodies flung into the ocean with the effortless ease of disposing of waste. I still think of Ma Brenda, her fingers intertwined and tucked between her thighs when she spoke about getting a better job in Europe, her stare disconcertingly intense. She had spoken in a precise manner, taking great care to pronounce each word, and flashing the crisp pound notes in my face when she told me to imagine how much more of these I'd have if I went to Europe. I still could not decide when was the exact moment I knew I had been tricked. Perhaps it had been on the bus headed for Cotonou from Lagos, sitting next to the two other girls whom I had slept next to for the past two days in Ma Brenda's house and yet whose names I still did not know, a quiet Ma Brenda sitting next to us and watching us with a hooded gaze. Or it was, perhaps, on the coast in Libya, with all those skinny men sizing us up with merciless eyes, laughing at their own jokes and wielding heavy guns as though they were toys. Or then, maybe it was after I woke up, dizzy, feeling as though my limbs were tied to bags of dried beans, to find myself on the floor of a prison, half-naked, two pairs of worried eyes looking down on me. Her name was Tee, she said, and I was "welcomed" to the land of no return.

No one had hinted at what they wanted with us. The rumor flying around was that we would be resold as slaves across Europe. But it was over a year now since we had been brought here (some, like Tee, had been here much longer), and there were no sales going on. No indication that one might commence soon. There was, instead, a routine of deaths and burials and futile attempts at escape followed by gruesome murders. It was as though that was all the superintendent wanted: to keep us in this dungeon for long enough that the few brave ones who could no longer stand the confinement would attempt to escape and then be no more. It was to him, perhaps, some sort of game with which he amused himself. The sadistic bastard that he was, I could only guess that he enjoyed this game very much.

I had noted to Tee when I first arrived that the prison wasn't at all conventional, without metal bars to isolate us and restrict our movements, no visible twenty-four-hour surveillance to prevent escape. She had looked at me with a mix of sympathy and puzzlement. How could I not know the extent of the danger I was in? It was the first time she had talked to me about the brave ones, the women who had attempted escape through the underground tunnel. Most of them believed they could get out safely if they chose the perfect time, she said, but there were surely others who knew for certain that they would be murdered. That was what a long time here could do to you. It was Tee who woke me up the next time a corpse was paraded. The girl had a fixed smile on her face, her eyes gently closed, so that at first glance I thought she was asleep. She could not have been older than nineteen. Tee said she was lucky; at least she got to leave, even though in death. And for days afterward, I would try to reconcile the word *lucky* with her still form in the hands of the guards, the smile on her face radiating a serene peace that had eluded her in life.

"Who's Paafo?" I asked Tee.

She stared at me. "Paafo?"

"You kept calling the name in your sleep last night."

"Did I?" There was something about her sudden air of alarm, something about her quick averted gaze. "She's... a friend," she said, finally.

"Oh." Something didn't feel right. "From home?"

She nodded and shook her head at the same time, tracing abstract patterns on the floor with her feet, taking great care to avoid my eyes. I had almost given up on getting a reply when she looked up and spoke quickly, as though not giving herself a chance to hold back. "We met on the shores of Takoradi. We were brought here together."

The revelation took some time to register.

"But... where is she now?"

When Tee turned to look at me, I got my reply in her eyes, already filling up with tears. Paafo was one of the brave ones. "She died," I said, quite unnecessarily.

"No." For some reason, she appeared surprised that I would consider that a possibility.

"She escaped."

I stared at her, my mouth open for a long time, until I remembered to close it. "How could she...," I began, but I never got to finish, because just then the warder strolled past, slow-walking and stoop-shouldered, as usual, casting a lazy glance at us, a small, sly smile on his lips. There was a look in his eyes I could not comprehend. It disturbed me.

There was something innocent yet creepy about him, the warder. Nobody knew how he had come to be. He was as old as the prison itself, some said. Others said he had been one of the prison guards but had lost his position after falling out of favor with the superintendent. He served us tasteless meals in the evening, scooping each spoonful of watery soup with an almost melancholic slowness. He dressed sparsely, in knee-length shorts and a top worn so often it was impossible to decipher its original color. He spoke with deliberate effort, his hands making descriptive gestures as though the listener were hard of hearing. It was difficult to feel anything but sympathy for him, small and slight as he was, with a defeated air about him. He had uncanny eyes, tiny and quick, with a piercing—albeit nervous—stare that seemed to search through the very recesses of a person's soul. Ijeoma said eyes were the windows to a person's world. The warder's made me wonder. His left eye was partially blind, a whitish liquid always streaming from it, and he had the jittery demeanor of one wary of an unprecedented attack. He had a certain smell about him, one that lingered long after he was gone. It was a mix of decayed leaves and a musky, unaired room. I often wondered what I would encounter if I pried those eyelids open and stepped into his eyes, into his world.

"How did she leave?" I asked Tee later that night. We lay close to each other and, in the dimness, occasionally reached out for each other.

Tee snorted. "You think if I knew I would still be here with you?"

I exhaled, suddenly tired. She was right, of course. And yet there was something unfurling within me, a solid hope amid apparent bleakness. It was not at all impossible to leave this place alive after all. There was a first and a second person in me.

"Someone else left after Paafo," Tee added, as though she had just read my thoughts.

"Alive?"

She shrugged. "Possibly."

I was beginning to smile when something occurred to me. "How do you even know they escaped?"

She hummed thoughtfully. "Well, they just disappeared. And they didn't go through the underground tunnel. That's the only known route for escape." Her silence added *and death, of course.*

"Maybe they were found and killed?" I prodded. My own pessimism shocked me.

"No." She seemed so certain, and then she added, as an afterthought. "Even if they somehow died, it wasn't the work of the superintendent."

"How would you know?"

"I know the superintendent," she said. "If his men had done the killings, he would have been sure to bring back the bodies for us to see. If only to remind us that no one would ever leave this prison alive." She paused, chose her next words carefully. "The superintendent obviously suspects someone has devised a means to allow people to escape from here without going through his trap. He doesn't know for sure where this route is or who is helping them get out."

"You think someone is helping?"

"Well, what do I know? It is just difficult to believe Paafo left here without somebody's help, somebody close enough to the superintendent to devise a means of escape." She smiled, dreamlike. "And this person must have sworn her to secrecy. Otherwise, I don't see Paafo leaving this place without me. Don't you think?"

I nodded. I was thinking, but not about the impossibility of Paafo leaving here without Tee. Only the guards held the key to the official entrance. The few of them around were stone-faced, knotted up in their obvious disdain for us. I could not see any of them helping Paafo. Not to mention how obvious it would have been. How directly incriminating. I sat up to think properly. The idea came to me with such clarity that I almost smiled. There was only one person who could have done this without fear of incriminating himself. It was stupid of me to even consider the possibility of the warder orchestrating something this complicated and foolhardy. He brought to mind an invalid, better suited to a sickbed, not to serving meals to dozens of women. But from then on I found I could no longer think of anything but how to venture into the secluded area of the prison and pay the warder a visit.

He glanced at me just briefly before he looked away. If he was surprised by my presence in this out-of-bounds part of the prison, down the hall from our quarters, he did not show it. He was sketching something on a piece of paper, eyes narrowed, brow furrowed in concentration. I did not have a good sleep the night before and all my joints ached. I thought of walking up to him, but one could never tell with these people. He might perceive a threat and raise an alarm. My mind was blank, unable to form a plan to summon him to me. If I called to him, it might attract the attention of the guards, and wouldn't that scare him off instead? And then it happened, before I could even come up with a strategy. My legs gave way, with the sudden feeling of candle wax placed above a fire. They buckled and I fell to my knees. He looked up from his sketching and hurried over, holding a lamp to my face.

"Are you all right?"

His tone had a gentle timbre that made me imagine, for a brief moment, that he was a friend. I shook my head slowly. "My legs...," I murmured.

"Sorry. Sorry. You think you can stand?"

I nodded. He bent over to help me up, circling one arm around my waist and one palm firmly holding my arm. He was frail, and I tried hard to hold myself up so we didn't both keel over. He was leading the way to a nearby seat when I gripped his arm suddenly, with a firmness that forced him to turn and look at me, alarmed.

"I know what you did for Paafo," I whispered, enjoying the sudden feeling of recklessness.

He looked as though he had happened on an errant ghost. When he finally found his voice, it matched my whisper, trembled with disbelief. "What on earth are you talking about?"

I could barely make sense of his heavily accented English, but there was a soothing sensation I got from the certainty that he was going to help me eventually, what with the leverage I had over him. "Paafo," I said, holding his startled glare, a coy smile playing—hard as I tried, I could not stop this—over my lips. The man's wrinkled face, furrowed all the more from shock, cut a funny picture, and biting my lip was all I could do to prevent myself from bursting into laughter. "I know you helped her escape. And I know you helped the other girl escape. I don't know what you did exactly, but you will help me escape too."

His mouth dropped. His grip on my arm slackened. He was shaking so furiously, I worried he was convulsive. "Jesus Christ," he mumbled under his breath, like a prayer. "Listen…"

"Or… I will walk to the superintendent and your secret will be known to him." I felt like Jezebel. I was no good at threats or blackmails, and this one left a bitter aftertaste.

I noticed a sudden shift in him. He became relaxed, no longer looked like death. In fact, it seemed—it was hard to believe—that he was actually chuckling softly, regarding me casually, with the fond look one uses when indulging an unnecessarily naughty child. "You think that scares me?"

"What?"

He laughed again. The precise quietness of it made it even more chilling. "What could the superintendent possibly do to me?"

"You allowed his prisoners to escape. That calls for stringent punishment," I said. I was not quite sure. The man's apparent calm made me feel like I was preaching to the choir.

"No." He seemed greatly amused. He moved forward, as though he were confiding a salacious secret to me. "The thought of me doing something like this is unimaginable to the superintendent. As far as he is concerned, I am just an unfortunate old man wasting my last years here, waiting to die. He would never believe you."

There was a certified emphasis on the "never" that momentarily numbed me. A certain assurance. He brought a wrinkled palm to my face and tilted my chin upward so I was looking deep into his eyes. There was not a trace of the familiar warmth. The bad eye was rotating eerily and I feared for a moment that a maggot would jump out and slide into mine.

"You, on the other hand, would have to explain where you got your information from. Like you said, you don't know how exactly I helped the girls escape. But I fear you would have to tell the superintendent anyway. And it had better be a believable story, or…" He stopped and chuckled again, leaving the rest of the words hanging in midair. He did not have to continue. I knew the rest. I thought of those women caught escaping, the story of how they had been stripped naked and whipped with horse whips and penetrated with broken bottles until they bled to death, how their bodies had been left to decay for days until they were finally taken out to be buried.

It was my turn to tremble. Something was coming undone in me, layers upon layers of gut wearing thin until I was overwhelmed with an emptiness, lightheaded. The voices in my head were screaming too loudly, blurring my vision, making the ache in my joints almost unbearable. The warder was moving away, his slow figure gradually fading from my vision.

"I'll do anything you want," I said. It was a mumble, so low I could have been soliloquizing, but he stopped, seeming undecided, and then he turned to me again. The look in his eyes had been replaced with something I could not pinpoint. It made me nauseous.

His features betrayed a coy smile. "You mean… anything?"

I could not form a clear picture of me beneath him, writhing and moaning, grasping and clutching his frail frame to myself. I could not think of moving in rhythm to match his weak thrust, all the while inhaling that stale smell that emanated from him. But I could think of the aftermath; I could see my mother bending down and scooping sand to throw at me, a confirmation that I wasn't a ghost. I could hear Ijeoma sobbing softly in my ears, murmuring over and over, "We thought we lost you. They told us you were dead." I could feel, for the very first time, the solidity of my freedom.

"Yes." I forced the word from my throat, let it float above me. "Anything."

The warder called it simple, but when he was done explaining the plan, I could not breathe. I became aware only of his hands on my arm, shaking me gently, his concerned face up close. I blinked him into focus, waited for my brain to fully understand. He was still in one piece, still the same smallish, smiling man with that nervous air. His peculiar smell filled his room, where he'd ushered me while the others slept. His left eye was still filmed and oozing whitish liquid. Nothing had changed. Those words had not just been my imagination.

His voice was smooth and mechanical as though reciting a memorized monologue. "Your chance of escape will come when the next prisoner dies. I believe that won't be so far away. I need you to be on alert. Always listen for the ringing of the bell. When the bell is rung, head for the coffin room. You have to climb into the coffin and lie next to the corpse and wait. Do not make a sound. Don't dare make even the slightest movement when the undertakers are in the room or taking the corpse out to be buried. Lie still. If it would help, fall asleep. And remain that way until you are buried alongside the corpse..."

I finally found my voice. "What?"

"Yes. You have to be buried."

I stared at him, surprised at my own calm, waiting for his laughter. It did not come. It took me several moments to realize he was serious. His idea of an escape from this place was being buried alongside a corpse. It occurred to me that he might not really be sane, and I suddenly wanted, more than anything, to maneuver my way toward the exit, just in case he went wild and charged at me. He only stood and stared back at me. There was something both vaguely disorienting and reassuring about his expression.

"…and this is where I come in," he continued, without a touch of unease. "You would be buried by evening, around eight o'clock, if I am not mistaken. All you have to do is wait. I'll come for you once it is past midnight, dig you up, and set you on your way. Okay?"

No, I wanted to say, but I seemed, at that moment, to have lost the ability to speak. The warder apparently took this as acquiescence, because he smiled, as though relieved that a huge task had been executed quite easily after all.

The coffin is lowered with a thud. Respect for the dead is apparently not their thing. I imagine myself as the corpse, rising up at this point, angered by the disrespect, to teach these men a lesson or two. But then what would I do to a living human beside me who was trying to take advantage of my death to escape? The thought makes me shudder. I sigh. It is best not to think about these things.

The first heap of sand lands moments later without warning, invading my solitude so suddenly that I nearly cry out in shock. A part of me contemplates, not for the first time, pushing the lid open to face these men. But would they be fooled into thinking I was the dead woman's ghost? Even if they were, would they be horrified enough to run away? I weigh the possible outcomes before I shake my head firmly. Those guards did not cut a picture of people who were afraid of ghosts. Moreover, if I escape now, then what? Where do I go from here? At least the warder would tell me what to do. It is best to wait until midnight.

"Take this torch."

"I can't do it…"

"I'm afraid you don't have a choice. It's either that or you remain here forever."

I shut my eyes, and for a moment hoped in vain to banish the image of a dead body, a strange one, for that matter, next to me. I wished there was a way to stop my fingers from shaking, wished I could form the words to make this man see why there had to be another way.

"But… what if I don't survive long enough for you to rescue me?" I asked.

"The others did. It's up to you to try as hard as you can to stay alive and fit for the journey ahead."

"What if… what if you don't make it out to come to my rescue?" I said, and immediately wished I hadn't. I could only hope he had not gotten my insinuation.

He had. He paused, tilted his head to the side to observe me closely. I saw something come alive in him, something light and tender. Or perhaps it was just my imagination. He moved forward, uncertainly, and ran a crooked finger across my cheek. "I don't play pranks, dear girl. You fulfilled your own end of the bargain and I will fulfill mine."

I resisted the urge to move away from him. The feeling of his fingers made my skin crawl.

"Now take the torch. You'll need it after I've dug you up. It'll be midnight, so you'll need something to find your way around that forest."

In the brief moment when our hands clasped around the torch, I looked up to meet his gaze. He was smiling at me. Without thinking, I smiled back.

*   *   *

I open my eyes slowly and wait for them to adjust to the darkness. I do not need a wristwatch to know that it is past midnight. The warder would not fail me. He was too good, too pure to go against his word, I tell myself. I am breathing these words, reveling in the small bouts of hope they bring, but I am unable to control the racing in my chest. My palms are sweaty, a bad sign, and my head woozy with grotesque imaginings. What if he fails to turn up? What if this has been a trick all along? What if Paafo and the other woman never escaped at all?

I close my eyes and try to slow my breath. I am thinking too much. To calm myself, I think of Ijeoma, try to picture her face with that smile that drew me to her years ago, try to imagine her soft nakedness against mine, only a few days from now. But it is hard to feel anything at all when you are lying next to a dead body, her smooth skin hard and cold, strangely soothing your unsteady nerves. Back in the coffin room, I had held the lid for a moment, mumbling a silent prayer to her chi, asking her spirit to forgive me and let me pass through safely. From the look of things, she had listened, had understood that we were all in this together and it was noble and honorable to assist each other in the little ways we could. I can only hope that she reasoned as I did: since she had not been of much use alive in that prison, it was comforting to be of use in death, unasked-for nonetheless. I wonder yet again who she is, and yet again something holds me back from turning on my torch, just within my reach, to see. The thought of leaving without establishing a bond burdens me with guilt. It seems to me a desperate moral obligation to memorize tidbits of information to go over in the forthcoming years. I can picture myself in a small studio flooded with light, a news correspondent sitting next to me, prodding me while I recount my experience. I try to think of the headlines that would go alongside the story, to think of the look on the superintendent's face when he sees it on the news. What would become of the warder afterward? Could my escape help secure the release of Tee?

I bite my lip. I ask too many pointless questions. I reach out, with a certain conviction that surprises even me, to clasp the woman's palm in mine. For some reason, I feel no fear, no awkwardness, only a familial kinship that unsettles me. I ache to run her palm along my cheek, to feel its deathly coldness against my damp forehead, to hold her palm in both of mine and preserve this bond until the scraping of a shovel arrives to deliver me to a new beginning. I fumble in my pocket for the torch. It is not there. I feel about me slowly, quietly, as though hitting vigorously might rouse the corpse. Just when I am starting to panic, my fingers close around the torch. I take a deep breath, bracing myself for the horror to come.

It is just then that it hits me: the smell, so forceful that I pause to blink, twice. It fills my nostrils, finding its way to my lungs, threatening to choke me with its familiarity. I realize with alarm that I am struggling to breathe. A queasiness envelops me, and when it lifts, I can hardly move my body. The darkness of the coffin has a new kind of menace. Ijeoma often says I have a quick mind, and so it takes me just a second to fit the puzzle together, and when I do, I cannot help the smile that stretches my lips. Something is rising up from beneath my stomach, tugging at my throat, threatening to break forth with abandon. I find it is laughter. Because then, when you are caught in a situation like this, what else could you possibly do but laugh?

The last thing I probably remember, just as my torch comes on and falls onto the face of the corpse, is the suffocating smell of decayed leaves and a musky, unaired room.

His eyes are vacant, as always, the liquid popping out like sour condensed milk.

I am forced to admit that even in death, the warder radiates the nervousness of one wary of an unprecedented attack.

FADING LIGHTS

by NGOZI JOHN

TONIGHT, I'M IN THE city of lights. Tonight, I'm lying on the bonnet of an old Mercedes, a pack of cigarettes in one hand, an unopened bottle of Smirnoff vodka propped on my stomach by my other hand. Tonight, I'm dying and my mind finds only one song to play, only one line of a song to repeat, for nothing. Just because I have to have something in my head.

I am in this city. The place where my body was the lightest. Where I let myself be carried like paper in a whirlwind, dancing round and round until my feet learned the tingle on their own. Until I was a little dizzy. A little drunk. A little mad. Laughing at myself. First, holding the laughter in my palm like a girl's coy giggle. Then letting it fall between my fingers and, when it hits the floor, shatter into tiny pieces of jumping lights that bounce back at me, kissing me in places that tickle and I'm overcome, throwing my head back and clapping and skipping and crying. This place where I became a paper boat on water, swaying softly. Peaceful. Peaceful. I chose this city because it is the only one that deserves my body.

I'm in Ibadan. It's 1993 and I'm Whitney Houston singing "I Will Always Love You." My six-year-old figure is drowning in my mother's buba. The lace is scratchy against my skin and the hem gets between my feet and slows down my glides, throws me over sometimes, but I get up, tighten my grip on a blue torch—my microphone, today.

"Adetoun!" My mother shouts my name from the kitchen. I hear the final clang of ladle against rim of pot, which indicates that lunch is ready.

"Adetoun, wa jeun o." She coughs and I know she just doused the fire from the kerosene stove and the smoke from it is filling her eyes with water.

It is the last part of Whitney's song and I have to finish, so I whisper and let the lines run into one another, missing the beats, so that my mother doesn't shout my name a third time. I'm out of the dress when she calls my name again.

My father is sitting at the head of the dining table when I get to the orange curtain that separates the sitting room from the dining space. His seat is turned to face the window and his head is thrown back against the chair. The curtain is drawn apart, his face catching the rays of sun streaming in. His eyes are closed and his fingers drum lightly on his thighs. He is arched toward the sun as though his body were sucking in its light and I know it's God sitting on his throne. My mother comes out of the kitchen carrying a tray of food and sits on his left, so I quickly step out from behind the curtain and climb into a chair. When my father turns around, the sun is sitting in his eyes and he's smiling down on me, on my mother, on the plates of rice and beef stew. His hands are resting on the table, his elbows bent out away from his body and his fingers splayed on each side of his plate as though he were saying, *Look at all I made.*

My mother makes to touch his hand at the same time as he pushes his chair back. The sound of it scraping the tiled floor leaves a sensation in my teeth and I see my mother stifle a sigh. It is when he rises that I remember how tall he is; how it has been months since I saw him; how his Afro is bigger and more unkempt than the last time he came home and his sideburns are untamed, crawling onto the middle of his face. His khakis stop mid-thigh, revealing coarse hair all the way down to his ankles, and his upper body strains against a singlet, which leaves his nipples peeking out from the sides.

"Wait. I have something for you." The smile is still in his eyes as he wags his finger at me. He pushes the chair in and taps my mother's shoulder before he disappears behind the curtain.

My mother sits in the chair like a mannequin for some minutes, then she squeezes my hand. "Eat your food." Her voice is a croak.

The steam from the rice carries the sweet aroma into my nose as I stir the stew into it. When my father returns, it is with a man's voice spilling from a cassette player. The man sings in a language I don't understand. His voice is a mix of love and sadness. My father sings along with him, places the radio on the table with a low thud that makes my mother flinch. He spreads his arms, throws his head back, glides across the room, sings in an exaggerated baritone that shapes his mouth into an O, starts the lines a little earlier than the singer, and hums the parts he doesn't know.

I want to stand up and dance with him but my mother is just sitting there looking at him with exasperation. The singer has switched to English now and his voice has lost its sadness. He sings about his daughter, whom he's giving out to her lover, about how hard it is for him to let her go. My father breaks into a dance. Claps his hands, shakes his shoulders, sidesteps. He looks ridiculous in his short khakis and tight singlet, moving like an earthworm. It makes my mother laugh, shake her head, so I laugh too.

"It's Nel Oliver," my father shouts above the music. "Fan*tas*tic singer." He draws out the second syllable of *fantastic*.

There's a lady in the song screaming at the top of her voice like she's seen a snake. I start to mimic her; it makes my mother laugh harder. My father dances toward me, carries me out of the chair, and spins me around. By the time I'm in his arms, the singer has reverted to his ballad, this time in Yoruba. So my head is just resting on my father's shoulder and I can smell the shea butter in his hair and my mother is wiping laugh tears from her eyes and Nel Oliver's voice is filling the room and my father's arms are wrapped around me, rocking me slowly, and it's God dancing with me.

This image of my father dancing in khakis and a singlet is the one I hold for the following seven years that I don't see him. It is this image that I push to the front of my mind when my memory of him threatens to be consumed by the picture of him kicking my mother in the face repeatedly with the heel of his brown shoe the next morning as she holds on to his right foot, begging him to stay.

That wasn't the first time he left. In the previous years, I had woken up to his sudden absence, to my mother's labored sobs at night, asking God to bring him back to her. I had seen my mother pack all his cassettes into a carton, crying over them and flinging them into it or setting them gingerly in rows, holding each one for too long, as though she were caressing the memory of him, sealing the carton with Sellotape as if it meant sealing off his memory.

With each of his absences came silence, silence so grave the floors refused to give sound to feet and the curtains became iron because the air liaised with the silence, and only the groan of the ceiling fan rebelled against it. And just the way he left, he returned. I would come home from preschool and he would be sitting there on the couch as though he had never left, head thrown back, eyes closed, listening to the music serenade the sitting room, the stack of cassettes sitting on the shelf as though they'd been there all along.

The first time I learn to fly, it is to make a star. I am twelve and a stone sits in my chest when my name is not announced as the winner of a singing competition in my church. I stand up and leave the hall as the girl I lost to moves to the stage to receive her prize. When I step outside the church, the day has rolled onto its back and parents are fighting the encroaching darkness with kerosene lamps, shouting the names of their children to call them in for the day. I don't stop walking until the night comes alive with light. Yellow streetlights; lights from moving cars; lights from sex workers' sparkly dresses and from sticks of cigarettes hanging between the lips or fingers of loud men; from fires stoked with sticks by roadside women or their children; blue, green, and yellow lights hanging on lines above the doorposts of nightclubs and bars. I follow these lights until the stone in my chest dissolves. When I get to my house's dark street, the moon has come out in a crescent and the stars are freckles of light around it. I imagine that a little finger reached to the sky and dotted it with each touch of its tip. I unwind my scarf from my head and tie it above my elbow, leaving a long tail for a wing. Then I spread my arms to the sky. My forefinger is pointing to the sky, just touching it with the tip, making stars. I'm running, I'm jumping, I'm skipping, I'm shooting stars from my fingertip. I'm flying.

My mom is pacing the sitting room when I get home. She rushes toward me as soon as I open the door and turns me round and round to check my body for any sign of distress.

"Kilo se e? Adetoun, nibo lo lo? Where did you go? Are you hurt? Why is your scarf on your arm? Did anything happen?" The questions tumble out of her. She draws me to her before I can answer and pushes me back again to examine me. "Where did you go?"

"I didn't go anywhere. I walked." I'm suddenly tired and I move to sit on the couch. Her eyes follow me.

"Why did you walk? Why didn't you wait for me in church?" She moves to the seat opposite me.

"Mummy, nothing. I just felt like walking. I even forgot you were in church," I lie.

The look on her face is one of confusion and fear. She gets up and stands over me. "Se you have started your own? You have started your own, too, abi? You felt like walking. Walking to where?" She sighs. "Just continue o. You people should kill me." Then she storms off into the bedroom, unable to give name to her fear, as though if she spoke it, it would become a breathing thing.

I am thirteen the next time I see my father. He is sitting in the cane chair on the veranda when I come back from school. He stands when he sees me, spreads his arms, and waits for me to walk into them.

"My angel." His smile is bright, oblivious to the pain in my heart.

I walk to him and give him a side-hug. My head stops short of his heart. I step back to observe him. His skin is darker and his hair has more gray.

I look toward the front door. "Where's Mummy? Has she seen you?"

"Yes. Oh yes. She's inside. She does not want to be bothered." He looks around frantically, searching for something, touches his pockets, finally finds them with his eyes.

"I just came to drop these." He picks a polythene bag from the floor beside the chair, opens it to reveal cassettes.

"Are you staying this time?" I try to hold his gaze.

He clasps my shoulders. "There's a concert in Lagos. It's Felabration."

I shrug out of his grip. "You have not come home for seven years." My voice quavers against my will.

"I know. I know, my darling." He cradles my face in his palms. I close my eyes.

"Will you come with me? Have you ever been to a music concert?" His eyes light up.

"I can't." I look up into his eyes, tears threatening to slither down my cheek. "I can't. Mummy…"

"Of course. Of course." He swings his hands, stuffs them into his pockets, bends to give me a kiss on my forehead, and walks out of the house.

I stand there, my vision blurred by tears, pressing down the pain in my heart and envious of his ability to just get up and leave.

It's 2006, the year I fall in love. First, with Sade Adu and the air that is her voice. Air that strips you of your clothes, of your fears, of your pain, and wraps itself around you like a soft blanket. Then I fall in love with a boy at the University of Benin. This is how we fall into each other. Me first. Although he would insist later that he was the one who saw me first across the hall. He would tease me about how my laughter was louder than Tony Tetuila's voice booming from the speakers, and how he thought I was annoyingly happy. "Jumping thing" is how he would describe me.

But I see him first. Not really him. The drabness. How when he walks into the hall in a group of four guys, he's looking like he walked into the wrong party. How he scowls at the cupid balloons hanging from the ceiling, ducks under the banners with VALENTINE'S DAY and I LOVE YOU printed on them. How he turns his face away when a girl from my table winks at his group, and is relieved when he sees an empty chair, which he quickly sinks into. How even among his friends, he manages to be alone. The bored expression. The rolling of his eyes every time the fat one in the red shirt laughs and slaps the table. The constant opening and flipping of the pages of the book in his hands. The carelessness of his shirt drooping over his leanness. The way he crosses his right leg over his left knee as though he were above everyone else. It amuses me, intrigues me, pulls at my curiosity until I find a seat beside him. I see him roll his eyes when I sit beside him and it makes me laugh.

I lean forward to shout above the loud music, "You brought a book." He shrugs.

"What's the title?"

He shows me the front cover. *This House Has Fallen* by Karl Maier. I don't know much about books.

"Well, is it interesting?" It's the chorus of the song and the crowd is singing along. It makes me strain my voice more.

He starts to speak, reconsiders, and takes a pen out of his breast pocket. I watch in amusement as he scribbles on the blank last page of the book. He pushes his book toward me. He has written his reply.

"Better than this party. I hate Valentine's Day."

I throw my head back in laughter and write my response. And he draws me into him, making me his accomplice. We laugh at the fat guy together; I agree with him that the rice tastes like candle; we roll our eyes when a guy proposes to his girlfriend, scrunch our noses at her exaggerated surprise. And when he writes, "There's this place where I eat isi ewu—" the sentence unfinished, I write back, "Yes."

I kiss him before I know his name. Okungbue, the one the sea owns.

*   *   *

This is how I lose him. First, I lose myself. I become a feather drowned in water. He is the water. I start by reading his books so I can argue with him when he talks about postcolonial disillusionment; by sitting with him on Somorika Hills to watch birds; by putting less pepper in food because of his ulcer; by following him around for his SUG presidential campaign; by accepting his weeks of silence and pretending to understand the need for space. I stand aside to let him in on the days when he appears at my door, watching him pace my room and complain about political consultations sucking his pocket dry, running my hands over his back soothingly when he finally collapses on my bed, subdued. In return, he hangs my picture on the wall in his room and calls me his anchor.

I lose him on the day he loses the SUG election. He rolls himself into a stone and sits on my heart until it crumbles from the pressure and I'm a wrung-out cloth.

It's night in Calabar and I'm in a hotel room lying on top of a man whose name I can't pronounce.

"It's Akpanudo." His breath smells like carbide.

"I don't give a fuck."

I roll off of him, pick up a shirt from the floor, and stand naked in front of the mirror on the wall beside the wardrobe. The ribbon that held my hair up in a puff has come undone and each end is hanging down the sides of my face. I tuck them back in. I don't stay long enough in front of the mirror to examine myself.

"You have to go. I have to meet my friends downstairs in an hour. I need to get ready." I throw his clothes onto him.

"The sex was good." He sits up and puts one leg into his trouser. "Will I see you again?"

"We are leaving tomorrow."

"Where's your school again?"

"UNIBEN."

"So what are you guys doing here?"

"Road trip."

"Wow. That's interesting. So will I see you again?"

"Sorry, I really need to get ready."

I sit in the bathtub and wash his scent off my body.

On the night my father dies, I learn that lights are fading things. I am sitting in a bus that smells like smoked fish. I stick my face out the window. I'm on my way to Ibadan because my mother sent me a text message.

"It's your father. He's not well. You should come home."

I hear the other things she does not say in the message:

You have not come home in four years.

You have become a drifter like him.

Was I the one? Did I push you away?

Things she said to me at the end of every phone conversation for the first two years, before the calls started to thin upon realizing that for her I would never be an open door. It was easier to be three states away, drifting—in my body, in people, in places too cold to call home—than to sit across from her in the living room as she put her fear between us, because letting herself have me held the promise of loss. It was easier than the day that, when I refused to follow her to a deliverance session with her pastor, she looked into my eyes and willed a demon out of me.

*   *   *

My father is lying in my mother's bed in a room that has forgotten his scent. It is hard to tell whether his eyes are open or closed. I kneel beside him and touch his arm. My mother is standing by the door, just watching, as if it were a stranger lying in her bed. My father is now a bony frame. His eyes are sunken, his lips are parched, and his skin has lost its light. He stirs when I touch his arm, turns his head slightly toward me, and smiles.

"You're here." He tries to push himself up. I help him up and prop his back with a pillow. "Have you now attended any music concert?"

I'm smiling and crying when he says this. I shake my head.

"I brought something for you." He slips his hand under the pillow by his side, brings out a flyer, and puts it in my hand. It has OLD-SCHOOL NIGHT printed in bold red alongside today's date. "You should go to this thing."

"This is why you came home?" I want my voice to carry all the pain seared upon my skin by people who turned my temple into a den of thieves, but it betrays me.

He puts his hand over mine. Lights flicker in his eyes, hints of the sun that once sat in them.

"I'm dying." His smile is sweet sadness. "I'm dying." This time he says it with an air of fulfillment and I see that he is a firefly, content with its own light. Consumed by its own light. He squeezes my hand. "You should go. It's not far away from here."

When I step into the club, I'm in heaven. James Brown's "I Feel Good" fills the hall. Disco lights hanging from the ceiling flash red, blue, yellow, green. People dressed in old-school costumes litter the open space. Ladies wearing checked skirts and cropped blouses, Afro wigs on their heads, men wearing pants with funnel hems, held up by suspenders over striped shirts, swinging each other around and shaking their shoulders and tapping their feet. I turn around to take it all in and bump into a dancing couple. I'm standing between them, trying to move out of their way, when they hold hands around me and start to swing. Another couple joins them and soon there's a circle around me. There are bubbles in my tummy. So I start to tap my feet. Slowly at first. Then faster. Tap. Tap. Tap. And I start to clap my hands. Down low. Up high. Down low. Up high. Then I'm shaking my shoulders forward and backward. Wriggling like an earthworm. Then I start to skip. And laugh. And skip. And cry. And jump. I'm skipping and clapping and laughing and crying and spinning and spinning and the colors from the disco lights are washing over me.

When the music stops, a lady climbs onstage. Her voice is water. She's singing Sade Adu's "King of Sorrow." The water carries me with it and I'm a paper boat, swaying softly in the night.

The lights are still on when I get home, and I can hear crying in the sitting room, my mother's groans as though there were fire in her throat, voices telling her to be strong.

God gives and takes away.

It's like someone poured a bucket of ice over my head, and I do not realize I have stopped breathing until my hand drops from the doorknob and I turn back to the road from which I came. It's almost midnight and the streetlights are lonely. Only a few cars speed past me. The lights from the cigarettes have been crushed by tired soles. The lights from the fires have been left to die out by sleepy women and children. The lights from the kerosene lamps have been turned down. There's a woman selling alcohol, cigarettes, sweets, and kola nuts under a tree in front of a mechanics' shop. I buy a bottle of Smirnoff vodka and a pack of Benson & Hedges.

I'm lying on the bonnet of an old Mercedes in the mechanics' shop. The sky is bare, like someone stole all its lights and hid them in a bag of clouds. Like it's mourning my father. I imagine his soul as rays of light shooting out through perforations in his body, lifting to the sky.

A line from Sade Adu's "King of Sorrow" is playing in my head.

I wonder if this grief will ever let me go.

My mind is on repeat, soaking up the grief and spreading it through my body. I come down from the car and I am moving to the music in my head until I become one with it, one with the grief, one with the sky, with the night, with this city. Until I'm floating.

I walk to the edge of the road. When I see a car coming, I start to step into the street. I pray it is a drunk driver. I pray he drives off and doesn't try to save me. But he sees me early and swerves too sharply so he grazes the curb. I start to laugh because he's so scared of death. Because he doesn't see that bodies are breaking things anyway that cannot be put back together.

He throws a curse at me, "God go punish you." His voice is a mix of fear and anger. And I'm laughing and laughing because God's body is lying in my mother's bed, broken.

CHIMAMANDA NGOZI ADICHIE grew up in Nigeria. Her work has been translated into thirty languages and has appeared in various publications, including the *New Yorker, Granta, The O. Henry Prize Stories*, the *Financial Times*, and *Zoetrope*. She is the author of three novels: *Purple Hibiscus* (2003), *Half of a Yellow Sun* (2006), and *Americanah* (2013), as well as a short-story collection, *The Thing around Your Neck* (2009). Her most recent work is *Dear Ijeawele, or A Feminist Manifesto in Fifteen Suggestions*.

OPE ADEDEJI dreams about bridging the gender-equality gap and destroying the patriarchy. She is a lawyer and editor. If you do not find her reading, you'll find her writing.

T. C. BOYLE is the author of twenty-eight books of fiction, including the novel *Outside Looking In* (spring 2019). "The Apartment" is his seventh story for *McSweeney's*, and it will be included in his next collection, along with stories from the *New Yorker* and *Esquire*.

DAWN DAVIES is the author of *Mothers of Sparta: A Memoir in Pieces* (Flatiron Books, 2018), as well as many other essays and stories. Her hobbies are free weights, poodles, and hair. Sometimes she teaches at writers' conferences. She lives in weird Florida.

MICHAEL DEAGLER's fiction has appeared in *Glimmer Train, KROnline, Electric Literature*'s Recommended Reading, and elsewhere. He has received fellowships from the Fine Arts Work Center in Provincetown, Massachusetts, and the Kimmel Harding Nelson Center for the Arts in Nebraska City, Nebraska.

ADACHIOMA EZEANO is an alumna of Purple Hibiscus Trust Creative Writing Workshop. Her work has appeared in *Brittle Paper, Deyu African, 9jafeminista, Critical Literature Review*, and elsewhere.

KATIE FARRIS is the author of *Boysgirls* (Marick Press) and the coeditor of *Gossip and Metaphysics: Russian Modernist Poems and Prose* (Tupelo Press).

MARY HOULIHAN is a comedian, writer, actor, and visual artist based in Brooklyn, New York.

GENEVIEVE HUDSON is the author of the story collection *Pretend We Live Here* (Future Tense Books, 2018), the hybrid memoir *A Little in Love with Everyone* (Fiction Advocate, 2018), and the forthcoming novel *Boys of Alabama* (Liveright, 2020). Her writing has been published in *Catapult*, *Hobart*, *Tin House* online, *No Tokens*, *Bitch*, the *Rumpus*, and other places. Her work has been supported by the Fulbright Program and artist residencies at Dickinson House, Caldera Arts, the Vermont Studio Center, and the MacDowell Colony.

CHUKWUEBUKA IBEH was born in Port Harcourt, Nigeria, in 2000. His short stories have been long listed for the Awele Creative Trust Short Story Prize and have appeared or are forthcoming in *New England Review of Books*, *Clarion*, the *Charles River Journal*, and elsewhere. He is an alumnus of the Purple Hibiscus Trust Creative Writing Workshop.

KRISTEN ISKANDRIAN is the author of the novel *Motherest*. Her short stories have been published in *The Best American Short Stories 2018*, *The O. Henry Prize Stories 2014*, *Zyzzyva*, *Ploughshares*, *McSweeney's*, *Tin House*, and many other places. She lives in Birmingham, Alabama, where she is working on opening an independent bookstore.

NGOZI JOHN studies English and literature at the University of Calabar, in Nigeria. In most of her writing, she explores individual struggle. She is interested in creating beautiful art experiences in Africa.

ILYA KAMINSKY is the author of *Deaf Republic* (Graywolf Press) and *Dancing in Odessa* (Tupelo Press).

SHUBNUM KHAN'S debut novel, *Onion Tears*, was shortlisted for the Penguin Prize for African Writing. She was selected as one of the *Mail & Guardian*'s "200 Young South Africans." She is the 2018 Jack Jones Literary Arts Retreat Octavia Butler Fellow. She lives in Durban, South Africa, and is working on a second novel and a collection of micro-memoirs.

DANIIL KHARMS was a Russian absurdist poet who was a cofounder of OBERIU movement. He died of starvation in Stalin's camps.

REIF LARSEN is the author of the novels *I Am Radar* and *The Selected Works of T. S. Spivet*, which was a *New York Times* best seller and was adapted for the screen by Jean-Pierre Jeunet (*Amélie*). Larsen's essays and fiction have appeared in the *New York Times*, the *Guardian*, *GQ*, *Tin House*, *Travel + Leisure*, *One Story*, the *Millions*, and the *Believer*. He currently lives in Troy, New York.

DANTIEL W. MONIZ is a homegrown Floridian whose work has appeared in *Tin House*, *Ploughshares*, and *Joyland*, among other publications. Her debut story collection, *Milk Blood Heat*, is forthcoming from Grove Atlantic.

MICHELLE TEA's latest book is *Castle on the River Vistula*, the final installment in her YA mermaid-y fantasy series. Her recent essay collection, *Against Memoir*, won the PEN/Diamonstein-Spielvogel Award for the Art of the Essay. She is the creator of Drag Queen Story Hour, among other things.

ROY UDEH-UBAKA exists between selves. When centered, he writes to them, for them, and about them. He is an alumnus of Chimamanda Adichie's Purple

Hibiscus Trust Creative Writing Workshop, and his stories have been published online in *Bakwa* magazine and are forthcoming in *Wasafiri*.

JOSE ANTONIO VARGAS is an author, journalist, filmmaker, and the founder of the nonprofit organization Define American.

EMERSON WHITNEY is the author of the memoir *Heaven*, forthcoming from McSweeney's in 2020, as well as the poetry book *Ghost Box* (Timeless, Infinite Light, 2014). Emerson teaches in the Bachelor of Fine Arts in Creative Writing program at Goddard College and is the Dana and David Dornsife Teaching Postdoctoral Scholar at the University of Southern California.

JINCY WILLETT is the author of the short-story collection *Jenny and the Jaws of Life* and the novels *Winner of the National Book Award*, *The Writing Class*, and *Amy Falls Down*. She is currently at work on a third Amy novel.

AVAILABLE FROM McSWEENEY'S

store.mcsweeneys.net

FICTION

The Domestic Crusaders .... Wajahat Ali

The Convalescent .... Jessica Anthony

Emmaus .... Alessandro Baricco

Mr. Gwyn .... Alessandro Baricco

Arkansas .... John Brandon

Citrus County .... John Brandon

A Million Heavens .... John Brandon

A Child Again .... Robert Coover

Stepmother .... Robert Coover

One Hundred Apocalypses and Other Apocalypses .... Lucy Corin

Fever Chart .... Bill Cotter

The Parallel Apartments .... Bill Cotter

Sorry to Disrupt the Peace .... Patty Yumi Cottrell

End of I. .... Stephen Dixon

I. .... Stephen Dixon

A Hologram for the King .... Dave Eggers

Understanding the Sky .... Dave Eggers

The Wild Things .... Dave Eggers

You Shall Know Our Velocity .... Dave Eggers

Donald .... Stephen Elliott, Eric Martin

The Boatbuilder .... Daniel Gumbiner
God Says No .... James Hannaham
The Middle Stories .... Sheila Heti
Songbook .... Nick Hornby
Bowl of Cherries .... Millard Kaufman
Misadventure .... Millard Kaufman
Lemon .... Lawrence Krauser
Search Sweet Country .... Kojo Laing
Hot Pink .... Adam Levin
The Instructions .... Adam Levin
The Facts of Winter .... Paul Poissel
Adios, Cowboy .... Olja Savičević
A Moment in the Sun .... John Sayles
Between Heaven and Here .... Susan Straight
All My Puny Sorrows .... Miriam Toews
The End of Love .... Marcos Giralt Torrente
Vacation .... Deb Olin Unferth
The Best of McSweeney's .... Various
Noisy Outlaws, Unfriendly Blobs… .... Various
Fine, Fine, Fine, Fine, Fine .... Diane Williams
Vicky Swanky Is a Beauty .... Diane Williams
My Documents .... Alejandro Zambra

ART & COMICS

Song Reader .... Beck
The Berliner Ensemble Thanks You All .... Marcel Dzama
It Is Right to Draw Their Fur .... Dave Eggers
Binky Brown Meets the Holy Virgin Mary .... Justin Green
Animals of the Ocean: In Particular the Giant Squid .... Dr. and Mr. Doris Haggis-on-Whey
Children and the Tundra .... Dr. and Mr. Doris Haggis-on-Whey
Cold Fusion .... Dr. and Mr. Doris Haggis-on-Whey
Giraffes? Giraffes! .... Dr. and Mr. Doris Haggis-on-Whey
Celebrations of Curious Characters .... Ricky Jay
There Are Many of Us .... Spike Jonze
Be a Nose! .... Art Spiegelman

The Clock without a Face .... Gus Twintig

Everything That Rises: A Book of Convergences .... Lawrence Weschler

BOOKS FOR CHILDREN

Here Comes the Cat! .... Frank Asch, Ill. Vladimir Vagin

Benny's Brigade .... Arthur Bradford; Ill. Lisa Hanawalt

Keep Our Secrets .... Jordan Crane

This Bridge Will Not Be Gray .... Dave Eggers; Ill. Tucker Nichols

The Night Riders .... Matt Furie

We Need a Horse .... Sheila Heti, Ill. Clare Rojas

Stories 1, 2, 3, 4 .... Eugène Ionesco

Hang Glider & Mud Mask .... Jason Jägel, Brian McMullen

Symphony City .... Amy Martin

Crabtree .... Jon and Tucker Nichols

Recipe .... Angela and Michaelanne Petrella; Ill. Mike Bertino, Erin Althea

Awake Beautiful Child .... Amy Krouse Rosenthal; Ill. Gracia Lam

Lost Sloth .... J. Otto Seibold

The Expeditioners I .... S.S. Taylor; Ill. Katherine Roy

The Expeditioners II .... S.S. Taylor; Ill. Katherine Roy

Girl at the Bottom of the Sea .... Michelle Tea; Ill. Amanda Verwey

Mermaid in Chelsea Creek .... Michelle Tea; Ill. Jason Polan

NONFICTION

White Girls .... Hilton Als

In My Home There Is No More Sorrow .... Rick Bass

Maps and Legends .... Michael Chabon

Real Man Adventures .... T Cooper

The Pharmacist's Mate and 8 .... Amy Fusselman

Toro Bravo: Stories. Recipes. No Bull. .... John Gorham, Liz Crain

The End of War .... John Horgan

It Chooses You .... Miranda July

The End of Major Combat Operations .... Nick McDonell

Mission Street Food .... Anthony Myint, Karen Leibowitz

At Home on the Range .... Margaret Yardley Potter, Elizabeth Gilbert

Half a Life .... Darin Strauss

VOICE OF WITNESS

Throwing Stones at the Moon: Narratives from
Colombians Displaced by Violence .... Eds. Sibylla Brodzinsky, Max Schoening
Surviving Justice: America's Wrongfully
Convicted and Exonerated .... Eds. Dave Eggers, Lola Vollen
Palestine Speaks: Narratives of Life under Occupation .... Eds. Mateo Hoke and Cate Malek
Nowhere to Be Home: Narratives from
Survivors of Burma's Military Regime .... Eds. Maggie Lemere, Zoë West
Refugee Hotel .... Juliet Linderman, Gabriele Stabile
Patriot Acts: Narratives of Post-9/11 Injustice .... Ed. Alia Malek
Underground America: Narratives of Undocumented Lives .... Ed. Peter Orner
Hope Deferred: Narratives of Zimbabwean Lives .... Eds. Peter Orner, Annie Holmes
High Rise Stories: Voices from Chicago Public Housing .... Ed. Audrey Petty
Inside This Place, Not of It:
Narratives from Women's Prisons .... Eds. Ayelet Waldman, Robin Levi
Out of Exile: Narratives from the Abducted and Displaced People of Sudan .... Ed. Craig Walzer
Voices from the Storm .... Eds. Chris Ying, Lola Vollen

HUMOR

The Secret Language of Sleep .... Amelia Bauer, Evany Thomas
Baby Do My Banking .... Lisa Brown
Baby Fix My Car .... Lisa Brown
Baby Get Me Some Lovin' .... Lisa Brown
Baby Make Me Breakfast .... Lisa Brown
Baby Plan My Wedding .... Lisa Brown
Comedy by the Numbers .... Eric Hoffman, Gary Rudoren
The Emily Dickinson Reader .... Paul Legault
All Known Metal Bands .... Dan Nelson
How to Dress for Every Occasion .... The Pope
The Latke Who Couldn't Stop Screaming .... Lemony Snicket, Lisa Brown
The Future Dictionary of America .... Various
I Found This Funny .... Various; Ed. Judd Apatow
I Live Real Close to Where You Used to Live .... Various; Ed. Lauren Hall
Thanks and Have Fun Running the Country .... Various; Ed. Jory John
The Best of McSweeney's Internet Tendency .... Various; Ed. Chris Monks, John Warner

POETRY

City of Rivers .... Zubair Ahmed

Remains .... Jesús Castillo

The Boss .... Victoria Chang

x .... Dan Chelotti

Tombo .... W. S. Di Piero

Flowers of Anti-Martyrdom .... Dorian Geisler

Of Lamb .... Matthea Harvey; Ill. Amy Jean Porter

The Abridged History of Rainfall .... Jay Hopler

Love, an Index .... Rebecca Lindenberg

Fragile Acts .... Allan Peterson

In the Shape of a Human Body I Am Visiting the Earth .... Various; Eds. Ilya Kaminsky,
Dominic Luxford, Jesse Nathan

The McSweeney's Book of Poets Picking Poets .... Various; Ed. Dominic Luxford

COLLINS LIBRARY

Curious Men .... Frank Buckland

Lunatic at Large .... J. Storer Clouston

The Rector and the Rogue .... W. A. Swanberg

ALL THIS AND MORE AT

store.mcsweeneys.net

ALL THAT IS EVIDENT IS SUSPECT:
READINGS FROM THE OULIPO, 1963–2018
edited by Ian Monk & Daniel Levin Becker

The first collection in English to offer a life-size picture of the group in its historical and contemporary incarnations, and the first in any language to represent all of its members

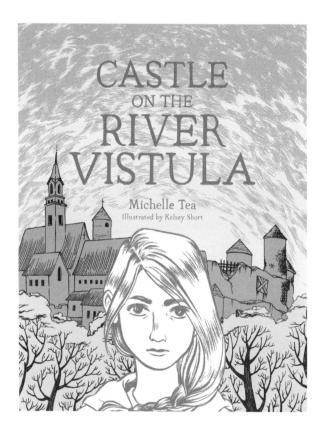

CASTLE ON THE RIVER VISTULA
by Michelle Tea

The final installment of Michelle Tea's groundbreaking
YA adventure series, the Chelsea Trilogy, here at long last

SORRY TO DISRUPT THE PEACE
by Patty Yumi Cottrell

"Sorry to Disrupt the Peace *is a debut that swaggers with the assurance of a fifth or even a tenth book." —Lauren Groff, from the judges' commendation for the Barnes & Noble Discover Great New Writers Award for fiction*

ALL MY PUNY SORROWS
by Miriam Toews

*"Irresistible… its intelligence, its honesty and, above all, its compassion provide a
kind of existential balm—a comfort not unlike the sort you might find by opening a
bottle of wine and having a long conversation with (yes, really) a true friend."
—Curtis Sittenfeld, the* New York Times Book Review

Founded in 1998, McSweeney's is an independent publisher based in San Francisco. McSweeney's exists to champion ambitious and inspired new writing, and to challenge conventional expectations about where it's found, how it looks, and who participates. We're here to discover things we love, help them find their most resplendent form, and place them into the hands of curious, engaged readers.

THERE ARE SEVERAL WAYS TO SUPPORT McSWEENEY'S:

Support Us on Patreon
visit *www.patreon.com/
mcsweeneysinternettendency*

Volunteer & Intern
email *eric@mcsweeneys.net*

Subscribe & Shop
visit *store.mcsweeneys.net*

Sponsor Books & *Quarterlies*
email *amanda@mcsweeneys.net*

To learn more, please visit *www.mcsweeneys.net/donate*
or contact Executive Director Amanda Uhle at
amanda@mcsweeneys.net or 415.642.5609.

All donations are tax-deductible through our fiscal sponsorship with SOMArts, a nonprofit organization that collaborates with diverse artists and organizations to engage the power of the arts to provoke just and fair inclusion, cultural respect, and civic participation.